Risk & Reward

To my brother Jon, who taught me everything I know.

Risk & Reward

How to handle market volatility and build long-term wealth

BEN CARLSON

 Harriman
House

HARRIMAN HOUSE
www.harriman-house.com

First published in 2026 by Harriman House, an imprint of Pan Macmillan
EU Representative: Macmillan Publishers Ireland Ltd, 1st Floor, The Liffey Trust
Centre, 117-126 Sheriff Street Upper, Dublin 1, D01 YC43
Associated companies throughout the world
www.panmacmillan.com
www.panmacmillan.com/ai-at-pan-macmillan

Paperback ISBN: 978-1-80409-326-9
eBook ISBN: 978-1-80409-327-6

British Library Cataloguing in Publication Data
A CIP catalogue record for this book can be obtained from the British Library.

02

Printed and bound by CPI Group (UK) Ltd.

Cover design by Charlotte Smith, based on a concept by Daniel Parra. Cover design
features human-edited AI imagery sourced from Adobe Stock.

CONTENTS

INTRODUCTION

**"Risk is what is left over... after you
have thought of everything."**

—CARL RICHARDS

L ET ME TELL you the secret to investing.

There is no secret.

Sorry to break it to you, but there is no Holy Grail that guarantees overnight riches in the markets. There's no confidential stock-picking scheme that will give you all of the upside with none of the downside. If there were an investment strategy that was guaranteed to work all the time it wouldn't be a secret and everyone would do it.

It has to be this way because risk and reward are attached at the hip. If you want to earn a return on your capital, you must accept risk in some form. One of the few iron laws of investing is there is no free lunch.

The first decade of the 21st century caused many investors to question their previously held beliefs. The stock market had barely recovered from the bursting of the dot-com bubble, which saw the stock market get cut in half from 2000 to 2002, before plunging nearly 60% during the Great Financial Crisis from 2007 to 2009. After a glorious bull market in the 1980s and 1990s, the 2000s were a lost decade of no returns with extraordinary volatility to boot.

That rough patch in the markets spawned a generation of

crash-callers and permabears. Everyone wanted to be the new main character in a Michael Lewis sequel to *The Big Short*. Investors went to a dark place after 2008 with a barrage of predictions about double-dip recessions, hyperinflation, a crash in the dollar and the end of the financial system as we know it.

Thankfully, none of those predictions came true, but being assaulted with constant crash predictions and warnings about it being a bad time to invest got me thinking.

What would happen if you only purchased stocks at the absolute peak of the market?

What if you had the worst luck and only invested at the top of the market before a Titanic-level disaster?

I wrote a piece on my blog, *A Wealth of Common Sense*, titled "What If You Only Invested at Market Peaks?" to answer this question using historical data. I wrote about a hypothetical retirement saver named Bob who held the unfortunate title of the world's worst market timer.

This was the premise:

- Bob would start saving for retirement at age 22 in the 1970s and retire at age 65.
- He would start by saving $2,000 a year and increase that amount by $2,000 each subsequent decade (for a total savings of $184,000 in 40+ years).
- Bob was a nervous investor so he would keep his money in a bank account until he could work up the nerve to invest in the stock market.
- Every time he bought stocks, he would keep his money invested in the market while his additional savings piled up in his checking account until he mustered up the courage to make another purchase.

Here's the catch – over his 40+ years of saving and investing, Bob's only stock market investments occurred just before four of the worst downturns in history:

- He invested $6,000 right before the 1973 to 1974 bear market which saw stocks tumble nearly 50%.
- He invested $46,000 right before the 1987 Black Monday crash which saw stocks crash 20% in a single day and 33% in a week.
- He invested $68,000 right before the 2000 to 2002 bursting of the dot-com bubble which saw stocks decline 50%.
- And finally, he invested $64,000 right before the 2007 to 2009 Great Financial Crisis which saw stocks plummet 57%.[*]

Bob made four of the most ill-timed stock market purchases in history. So how did he do? Bob retired a millionaire – $1.1 million to be exact – at age 65. How is this possible?!

Those ill-timed purchases and subsequent losses were painful to be sure, but the stock market recovered and eventually moved higher. Bob never sold a single share and slowly but surely increased the amount of money he saved over time. He felt the risk up-front and the reward many years later. Bob's results illustrate the power of compounding, consistency and long-term thinking in the markets. A long time horizon is the ultimate equalizer when investing, even when you're the worst market timer the world has ever seen.

I published that piece in 2014. It's far and away the most popular blog post I've ever written, with more than a million readers and counting. The benefits of long-term investing have really resonated with readers.

But there are plenty of detractors as well. The most significant counterargument looks something like this:

---

[*] Bob was also sitting on some cash since he didn't invest the rest of his savings after his last ill-fated investment in 2007.

NOW SHOW JAPAN! Sure this works in the United States but what about places like Japan where the stock market has gone nowhere for multiple decades? Doesn't your argument fall apart?

This is a fair criticism.

Winners write history books, and the U.S. stock market has been the big winner for over a hundred-plus years. In 1900, U.S. stocks made up just 15% of world equity market capitalization. By 2025, the U.S. stock market comprised 65% of world market capitalization.

Indeed, Bob would not have fared as well if he had invested exclusively in Japanese stocks. After topping out in 1989, Japan's stock market crashed and then went nowhere for three-plus decades. Investing money in Japanese stocks has been an awful investment experience since 1990.

However, "Now show Japan" doesn't necessarily invalidate an investment philosophy of thinking and acting for the long term. If anything, Japan is a wonderful case study in risk and reward (we will get to this in more detail in Chapters 15 and 16).

First things first – I believe in the power of compounding. I believe simple beats complex, less is more, costs should be low, behavior matters more than spreadsheets, diversification helps manage risk, and markets work over the long run. I don't try to predict the future, but I find it helpful to analyze the present and calculate probabilities from the past. I believe the long term is the only time frame that matters to investors, but you also have to survive the short term to experience the benefits.

I also believe it's essential to stress-test your most strongly held views regarding investing, business or anything else in life. This book plays devil's advocate on the entire premise of long-term investing. I take a wrecking ball to my own investment philosophy to look at the good, the bad and the ugly. Ultimately, I prove the reward is worth the risk, but the two are inextricably linked.

Winston Churchill once said, "Many forms of government have

been tried, and will be tried in this world of sin and woe. No one pretends that democracy is perfect or all-wise. Indeed it has been said that democracy is the worst form of government except for all those other forms that have been tried from time to time."

And so it is with investing.

Many forms of investing have been tried and will be tried. Long-term investing is not perfect or all-wise. Buy and hold is the worst form of investing, except for all those other investment strategies that have been tried from time to time.

In the climactic scene in the movie *8 Mile*, we're shown the final rap battle between Eminem's B-Rabbit and his arch nemesis, Papa Doc. I've never personally been in a rap battle, but I gather the point is to create some rhymes that denigrate your opponent while doing your best to get the crowd to wave their hands in the air from side to side like they just don't care.

Instead of taking shots directly at Papa Doc, B-Rabbit flips the script by belittling himself before his counterpart even has the opportunity. His self-deprecation wins over the crowd with lines like, "I know everything he's 'bout to say against me. I am a f***ing bum. I do live in a trailer with my mom."

Then he drops the mic with this finish:

Here, tell these people something they don't know about me.

The crowd goes wild. Papa Doc is left speechless with no rebuttals. The rap battle is over.

This book takes a similar approach to long-term investing. I lay out all of the risks from "Now show Japan" to the Great Depression to the lost decades and everything else that can and will go wrong in the markets. Then I provide context around those risks and offer solutions to help you survive the short term so you can thrive in the long term.

Peter Lynch once said, "The real key to making money in stocks is not to get scared out of them."

We live in a world in which you are bombarded with negativity everywhere you look – social media, the news, politicians, podcasts, alerts on your smartphone and the financial media. It's the new normal of negativity where pessimism gets the most eyeballs.

I've always been a glass-half-full person. I'm optimistic by nature. I believe the future will be better than the past because people wake up every day looking to better their station in life. That's why we get innovation, growth and prosperity. But I am not naive to the fact that there will always be setbacks along the way. The graph doesn't always move up and to the right in a straight line.

You are guaranteed to experience recessions, bear markets, financial crises, market crashes, geopolitical conflicts, war, pandemics, natural disasters and Black Swan events you can't even imagine. Despite all of these nightmarish scenarios I still believe investing over the long term is your best bet.

This book aims to help you better understand the risks involved in investing and give you the ammunition to stick around long enough to earn the rewards. By the end, you will have a better grasp of the biggest risks and how to protect yourself against them.

As Dolly Parton once said, "The way I see it, if you want the rainbow, you gotta put up with the rain."

Let's start by looking at some of the worst days, months and years in stock market history.

1.

IT WAS THE
WORST OF TIMES

"Most people get interested in stocks
when everyone else is. The time to get
interested is when no one else is."

—WARREN BUFFETT

S *HARK WEEK* PREMIERED on the Discovery Channel in 1988.
The series was originally about promoting the conservation of
sharks and clearing up any misconceptions about these enigmatic fish.
But that's not what the majority of viewers took away from the show.
As *Shark Week* grew in popularity, viewers became more concerned
about shark attacks because shark attacks make for good TV.

Researchers conducted a study on different groups of people to
examine how watching the show influenced their perception of sharks.
One group was shown footage of violent shark attacks, while the other
watched non-violent shark footage. The more exposure participants
had to violent videos, the more fearful they became of sharks. This
fear persisted even when public service announcements at the end of
each episode emphasized the rarity of shark attacks. Although *Shark
Week* was intended to be educational, viewers were primarily drawn to

the worst-case scenarios. People tend to disregard statistics, but react strongly to visuals of a massive predator with a menacing fin and sharp teeth capable of ripping you to shreds. Funny how that works.

Sharks are not the most deadly animals in the world – not even close. In fact, the most deadly animal in the world is actually the teeny-tiny mosquito, which kills hundreds of thousands of people each year. *Mosquito Week* just wouldn't have the same ring to it, but humans are far more likely to die from a mosquito bite than a reenactment of *Jaws*. Lightning kills almost 50 people a year, while deer accidents kill another 150 people or so. More than 300 people drown in the bathtub each year. Shark attacks account for around five to six deaths per year, on average. You can see the most deadly animals in Figure 1.1.

Figure 1.1: Number of people killed by animals (2015)

Animal	Deaths
Mosquito	830,000
Snake	60,000
Scorpion	3,500
Hippo	500
Elephant	100
Jellyfish	40
Shark	6

Source: Gates Notes.

Those other risks don't make for a very compelling story so people spend all their time worrying about the low-probability events they read about in the headlines.

I could really tie up this analogy into a neat bow if only there were another place where people misperceive the risks involved. A place where people are swayed by scary narratives and headlines, instead of paying attention to the evidence. A place where people fall prey to the constant drumbeat of scare tactics, noise, and clickbait to make decisions.

Wait a minute… that's the stock market!

The more shark attacks you watch, the more fearful you become of sharks. The same is true of the stock market. The more you focus on the downturns, the more fearful you become of them.

Let's take a look at all of the *shark attacks* that have occurred in the financial markets – the worst of the worst – to get it all out in the open.

First, Table 1.1 shows the 10 worst days in the U.S. stock market (represented by the S&P 500) going back to 1928.

Table 1.1: The worst days in stock market history (S&P 500, 1928–2024)

Date	Total Return
October 19, 1987	−20.5%
October 28, 1929	−12.9%
March 16, 2020	−12.0%
October 29, 1929	−10.2%
November 6, 1929	−9.9%
March 12, 2020	−9.5%
October 18, 1937	−9.1%
October 5, 1931	−9.1%
October 15, 2008	−9.0%
October 1, 2008	−8.9%

Source: S&P 500 from 1928–2024.

Black Monday on October 19, 1987 was the worst day in stock market history. The stock market saw one-fifth of its value evaporate in a single day. It's hard to explain how jarring this event was for investors at that time. Twenty percent of your money invested in stocks just vanished. The rest of the list includes days during the Great Depression, the 2008 Great Financial Crisis and the Covid Crash in 2020.[*]

Now let's take a look at the 10 worst months in U.S. stock market history, in Table 1.2.

Table 1.2: The worst months in stock market history
(S&P 500, 1928–2024)

Month	Total Return
September 1931	−29.7%
March 1938	−24.9%
May 1940	−22.9%
May 1932	−22.0%
October 1987	−21.5%
April 1932	−20.0%
October 1929	−19.7%
February 1933	−17.7%
October 2008	−16.8%
June 1930	−16.3%

Source: S&P 500 from 1928–2024.

Imagine you have a $1 million stock portfolio and suddenly a month later it's now worth $800,000 or $700,000. That's how quickly money can be vaporized in the stock market.

---

[*] For some reason, October is when the worst days tend to occur. Seven out of the 10 worst days occurred in the 10th month of the year.

The 1930s saw that happen in back-to-back months during April and May of 1932. In total the stock market was down almost 40% in the course of two months. Just brutal. It's hard to believe, but there have been just as many 20% or worse down months as there have been 20% or worse down years.

Table 1.3 shows the 10 worst years in U.S. stock market history.

Table 1.3: The worst years in stock market history (S&P 500, 1928–2024)

Year	Total Return	Event
1931	−43.8%	Great Depression
2008	−36.6%	Great Financial Crisis
1937	−35.3%	1937 Crash
1974	−25.9%	1973–74 Crash
1930	−25.1%	Great Depression
2002	−22.0%	Dot-Com Crash
2022	−18.1%	The Great Inflation
1973	−14.3%	1973–74 Crash
1941	−12.8%	WWII
2001	−11.9%	Dot-Com Crash

Source: S&P 500 from 1928–2024.

These tables are littered with the worst economic and financial environments in history. The bad times tend to cluster together. Three of the worst years took place during the Great Depression and its aftermath in the 1930s. There were also three big down years that took place during the first decade of the 21st century in 2001, 2002 and 2008. Financial crises and bad economic times lead to poor outcomes in the stock market that can be difficult to stomach.

When you experience these cash incinerators, the fluctuations can tempt you into making mistakes. Volatility in stock prices leads to volatility in your emotions. The severity of market crashes such as these over days, months, and years can make even the most disciplined investors question their investment sanity.

What if the market doesn't come back?

What if stocks keep crashing?

How am I ever going to recover from this?

Some investors can handle holding all of their investable assets in a 100% stock portfolio. If you have the correct emotional disposition and time horizon, you may be able to justify going all in on stocks. If you're going to invest your entire portfolio in stocks, you need to remain calm during the worst days, months and years. Every long-term investor will get tested in the short term.

The good news is that you can recover from these *stock attacks* if you can wait them out.

It was the best of times after the worst of times

The worst of times are painful but never last forever. Investing when stocks are down is a wonderful strategy because it usually leads to higher returns.

Table 1.4 shows what happened one, five and 10 years following the worst months in stock market history.

Table 1.4: After the worst months in stock market history (S&P 500, 1928–2024)

Date	Total Return	One Year	Five Years	Ten Years
September 1931	−29.7%	−9.6%	118.2%	84.7%
March 1938	−24.9%	35.2%	84.5%	207.1%
May 1940	−22.9%	8.0%	118.8%	263.8%
May 1932	−22.0%	131.3%	367.4%	218.1%
October 1987	−21.5%	14.7%	96.8%	387.1%
April 1932	−20.0%	54.5%	265.6%	130.0%
October 1929	−19.7%	−26.6%	−51.2%	−9.2%
February 1933	−17.7%	98.7%	154.6%	234.7%
October 2008	−16.8%	9.8%	102.6%	246.7%
June 1930	−16.3%	−23.4%	−32.8%	−15.6%
Averages	**−21.2%**	**29.3%**	**122.4%**	**174.7%**

Source: S&P 500 from 1928–2024.

Take a look at what happened following the 1987 crash. It was the fastest bear market in history. At the time people worried the market was signaling a repeat of the Great Depression. Yet stocks were up 15%, 97%, and 387% respectively over the ensuing one, five and 10 years. If you had the courage to buy in the midst of a panic, you were handsomely rewarded.

Good returns tend to follow bad returns. The price of admission to the stock market is bone-crushing volatility, a lumpy return stream and the anguish of witnessing a chunk of your life savings evaporate before your eyes. In exchange, you get long-term returns above the rate of inflation and compounding that can earn you multiples of your initial investment in the greatest wealth-building machine ever created.

Buying stocks when they're on sale

Despite all of the terrible losses you can encounter in the stock market over the short run, the long-term track record is still quite impressive. From 1928 to 2024, the S&P 500 achieved an annual return of 9.9% per year. Those returns include every one of the worst days, months and years outlined in this chapter.

In that time, the stock market was positive in roughly three out of every four years. The average positive year saw gains of around 21%, while the average down year was closer to a loss of 14%. Investing in stocks involves both big losses *and* big gains.

To keep things simple, let's use +20% for the up years and -15% for the down years since I like nice round numbers. If the stock market went on a four-year run with returns of +20%, +20%, +20% and -15%, the annualized return in these four years would be +10% per year.

Still with me?

Let's say you plan on saving $1,000 a year for the next 40 years and get this same return stream of gains every three out of four years. Now let's look at two different scenarios where the annual returns at the end are exactly the same:

- **Scenario A**: You get -15% annual losses in the first 10 years followed by 30 years of +20% annual gains.
- **Scenario B**: You get 30 years of +20% annual gains followed by 10 years of -15% annual losses.

If you're a periodic investor in the stock market, which scenario should you prefer?

In Scenario A, where your returns were dreadful in the first 10 years but wonderful in the ensuing 30 years, your final balance after 40 years would be $2.5 million.

In Scenario B, where your returns were wonderful in the first 30 years but dreadful in the final 10 years, your final balance after 40 years would be just over $200,000.

In each scenario, the market's average annual return is 10%, but the results are miles apart.

How can this be possible?

In Scenario A, you're saving and investing during your most important compounding years, when you're young, during a brutal bear market. In Scenario B, you're saving and investing during your most important years during a rip-roaring bull market. It's more advantageous to buy in at lower prices when you're young because compound interest takes time to work (more on this in Chapter 14).

Obviously, these examples are not realistic. If the stock market fell 15% for 10 straight years, that's a loss of 80%. Gaining 20% for 30 straight years would give you a return of nearly 24,000%.

But the point remains: If you are just starting out as an investor, the best thing that could happen to you is a series of down markets. You should get down on your hands and knees and pray to the god of Gordon Gekko that stocks will fall when you are putting more money to work in the market. When stocks go on sale you don't want to run out of the store, you want to lean into the pain and buy more!

Sometimes the worst of times can be the best of times. It all depends on your age, time horizon and place in life as a saver or investor. If you are saving money on a regular basis, lower stock prices are a good thing. It means you get to buy stocks on sale! Poor returns aren't always a bad thing as long as they lead to better returns down the road.

However, if you need to spend down a portion of your portfolio, or if you desire less volatility so you can sleep more soundly at night, then adding another asset class can help.

The 60/40 portfolio

Now that we've established the wild price swings you can see in the stock market, it's only natural to inquire what options you have besides gritting your teeth and sitting through big losses.

There are two ways to manage risk in stocks: you can diversify or you can extend your investment time horizon. Let's take a closer look at each of these forms of risk management.

Sometimes you diversify to control your emotions during short-term volatility. Sometimes you diversify because you have spending needs and don't want to sell stocks when they are down. And sometimes you desire a source of dry powder so you can rebalance into the pain when stocks are on sale.

Traditionally, the main diversifier for stocks has been bonds. To show how this works, let's look at the 26 years in which the U.S. stock market finished with a loss from 1928 through 2024. Table 1.5 provides a look at each of those down years along with the corresponding returns for U.S. Treasuries.

Table 1.5: Bonds help when stocks fall (S&P 500 and 10-year Treasuries, 1928–2024)

Year	Stocks	Bonds	Year	Stocks	Bonds
1929	−8.3%	4.2%	1966	−10.0%	2.9%
1930	−25.1%	4.5%	1969	−8.2%	−5.0%
1931	−43.8%	−2.6%	1973	−14.3%	3.7%
1932	−8.6%	8.8%	1974	−25.9%	2.0%
1934	−1.2%	8.0%	1977	−7.0%	1.3%
1937	−35.3%	1.4%	1981	−4.7%	8.2%
1939	−1.1%	4.4%	1990	−3.1%	6.2%
1940	−10.7%	5.4%	2000	−9.0%	16.7%
1941	−12.8%	−2.0%	2001	−11.9%	5.6%
1946	−8.4%	3.1%	2002	−22.0%	15.1%
1953	−1.2%	4.1%	2008	−36.6%	20.1%
1957	−10.5%	6.8%	2018	−4.2%	0.0%
1962	−8.8%	5.7%	2022	−18.0%	−17.8%

Source: NYU (S&P 500 & 10-year Treasuries).

The average return for stocks in these 26 down years was -13.5%. During those same years, bonds averaged gains of 4.3%, meaning that boring old U.S. government bonds outperformed stocks by nearly 18 percentage points on average when stocks finished the year down.

Diversification didn't work all the time. There were four years when stocks and bonds were both down in the same year.* Still, high-quality bonds have generally provided a ballast to a portfolio when stocks are getting bludgeoned.

Having seen the performance of bonds in the worst years for stocks, it makes sense that some investors opt for a combined portfolio of stocks and bonds. The 60/40 (60% in stocks and 40% in bonds) is the portfolio of choice for many investors who want exposure to the growth power of stocks, but also desire an offset.

Let's take a look at the worst years ever for a 60/40 portfolio (Table 1.6).

Table 1.6: The worst years for a 60/40 portfolio (S&P 500 and 10-year Treasuries, 1928–2024)

Year	Total Return	Event
1931	−27.3%	Great Depression
1937	−20.7%	1937 Crash
2022	−16.9%	The Great Inflation
1974	−14.7%	1973–74 Crash
2008	−13.9%	Great Financial Crisis
1930	−13.3%	Great Depression
1941	−8.5%	WWII
2002	−7.1%	Dot-Com Crash
1973	−7.1%	1973–74 Crash
1969	−6.9%	Nifty Fifty Crash

Source: NYU.

---

* The worst-case scenario was 2022, when bonds and stocks each got shellacked. High inflation and rapidly rising interest rates hurt both stocks and bonds that year. It can happen, but it's rare.

Many of the worst years for a 60/40 portfolio are the same as the worst years for the U.S. stock market. This makes sense, since the 60% in stocks carries much more risk than the 40% in bonds. It should provide some comfort to know that in the 97 years from 1928 to 2024, there were just six times when a 60/40 portfolio finished the year down double-digits. A 20% down year occurred just twice. There are no guarantees the future will be like the past, but these are pretty good historical odds.

Now let's look at the worst 10-year returns for a 60/40 portfolio. Table 1.7 shows the ending dates of 10-year periods and the total return of a 60/40 portfolio in that decade.

Table 1.7: The worst 10-year periods for a 60/40 portfolio (S&P 500 and 10-year Treasuries, 1928–2024)

Year Ending	Total Return
1938	19.5%
1939	25.0%
1937	26.9%
1974	27.3%
2008	31.3%
2009	33.5%
1940	38.0%
1946	45.5%
1975	46.1%
2010	48.8%

Source: Returns 2.0.

By my calculations, there has never been a negative return over 10 years for a 60/40 portfolio as of a calendar year-end. Could it happen? Absolutely. There is no such thing as always or never in the financial markets. But again, this is a good track record.

Finally, let's look at the worst 20-year returns for a 60/40 portfolio.

Table 1.8 shows the ending dates of 20-year periods and the total return of a 60/40 portfolio in those 20-year blocks.

Table 1.8: The worst 20-year periods for a 60/40 portfolio (S&P 500 and 10-year Treasuries, 1928–2024)

Year Ending	Total Return
1948	98.3%
1949	131.4%
1947	140.9%
1978	204.1%
1974	204.5%
2018	207.0%
1981	208.4%
1975	216.3%
1950	216.5%
1979	219.0%

Source: Returns 2.0.

As with most worst-case historical performance numbers, the starting point for the bottom of the barrel was 1929. With a total return of +98.3%, the 20 years from 1929 to 1948 saw an annual gain of 3.4%, where you doubled your money in total. That's not bad for a worst-case scenario.

Past performance is not indicative of future results, but sometimes it is helpful to zoom out when thinking about how bad things could get. Extending your time horizon remains one of the most powerful investment strategies when all else fails.

How to win

The win rate for a 60/40 portfolio over various time frames tells the story here too. Using rolling monthly returns, Figure 1.2 shows the improvement in win rates as you extend your time horizon.

Figure 1.2: 60/40 win rate by holding period (S&P 500 and 5-year Treasuries, 1928–2024)

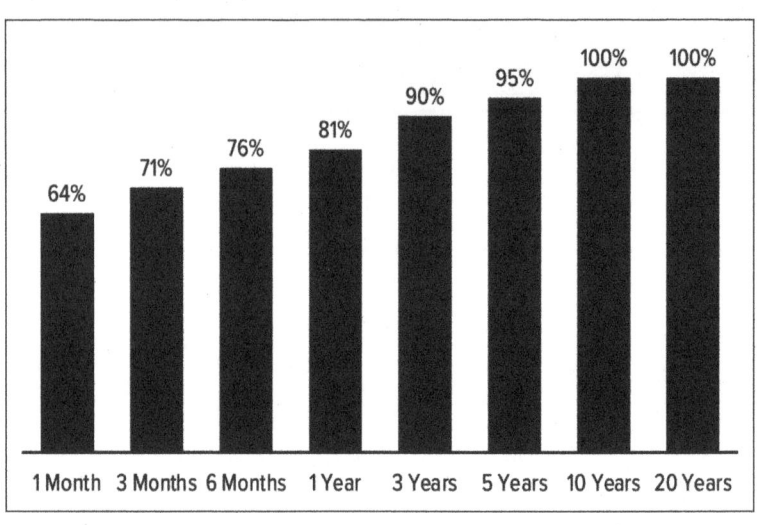

Source: Returns 2.0.

The data is clear – the longer your time horizon, the more likely you will experience positive results. Historically, if you held a 60/40 portfolio for one month, there is a 64% chance you would have had a positive return. If you held for 10 years, you were up 100% of the time.

Of course, a positive result doesn't guarantee a specific level of return. Figure 1.3 shows the historical rolling 10-year total returns for a 60/40 portfolio.

Figure 1.3: 60/40 portfolio rolling 10-year returns (S&P 500 and 5-year Treasuries, 1928–2024)

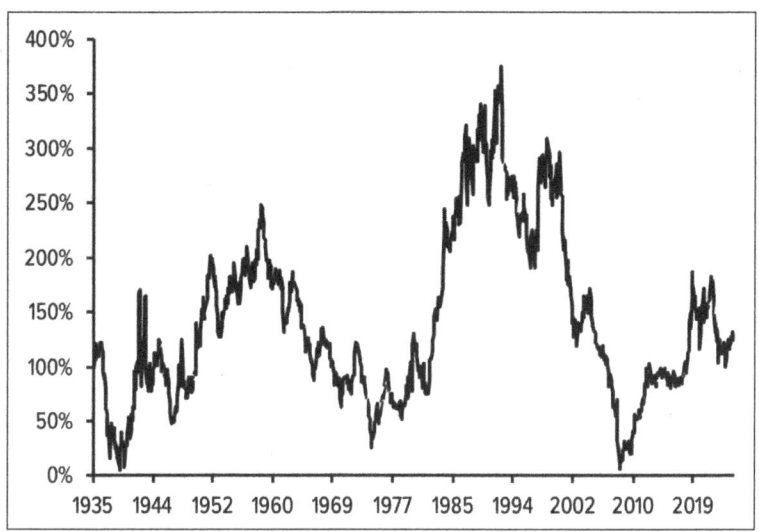

Source: Returns 2.0.

The returns tend to trend much lower during financial crisis periods in the 1930s, 1970s and 2000s. Some 10-year returns have been better than others, but the results have been impressive nonetheless.

Whether you have all of your money in stocks or a more diversified portfolio, long-term investing continues to give you the best odds of success in the markets.

Don't fixate only on the shark attacks. This is easy to say if you're reading this on a calm day in the markets when recent returns have been good. But remember it on the days, months and years when the market is falling too.

Stock market returns have been strong even with all of the bad daily, monthly and annul returns investors have experienced.

In the next chapter we'll look at why being a long-term investor can be so challenging.

2.

DOING NOTHING
IS HARD WORK

"The best investors make a habit
of putting procedures in place, in
advance, that help inhibit the hot
reactions of the emotional brain."

–JASON ZWEIG

THERE IS AN old parable about a locksmith who takes on an apprentice.

When the apprentice first starts out, he struggles at picking locks. If someone gets locked out of their home or car, it takes him a long time to pick the lock. He uses many tools and different angles to get the job done. By the time the door is open, he's practically sweating.

The clients see the time and effort he puts in, so they're generous with tips. Over time, the master locksmith teaches him the tricks of the trade, and with practice, the apprentice improves. He gets faster, and more efficient. Eventually, picking a lock becomes second nature. However, this creates a problem for his pocketbook because now the people who hired him don't think he's working so hard anymore. Even though the apprentice is more skilled at lock-picking, his tips go down and he makes less money.

It takes a lot of hard work up front to make it look easy.

Late-night host Jimmy Kimmel once proclaimed comedian Martin Short was the greatest dinner guest of all time and deserved to be on the Mount Rushmore of talk show guests. Short was once interviewed on the process he goes through in preparation for these guest spots:

What I do for a typical talk-show appearance, and I'm not exaggerating, is I'll send in something like 18 pages ahead of time.

They could start with an idea for an opening and then it could go to 'This story could work, and that story, and that story, and that story, and that story, and that story.' Then we whittle it down. I'll probably be on the phone with the segment producer for at least an hour-and-a-half going through ideas for material. Then you have to balance all that during the appearance by making it look improvised in the moment, not speaking too much, trying to find common ground with the host. Like if I'm doing Fallon's show, I'll make sure we talk about *SNL* for a bit.

Short distills nearly 20 pages of material and 90 minutes with a producer into a polished five-minute segment. During those five minutes, he describes his talk show appearances as "an impersonation of myself being relaxed." It comes off as if he's going off the cuff and improvising on the spot, but this is years and years of honing his craft to make it appear like a casual conversation.

Another example of this is Jerry Seinfeld's well-known bit about Pop-Tarts in his stand-up:

I don't know how long it took them to invent the Pop-Tart. But they must have come out of that lab, like Moses with the two tablets of the Ten Commandments. The Pop-Tart is here. Two in the packet. Two slots in the toaster.

Let's see you screw this up. Why two? One's not enough. Three's too many. And they can't go stale. Because they were never fresh!

Seinfeld told an interviewer he'd been working on this joke for two years before it was perfected. Two years!

You might assume stand-up comedians are naturally funny storytellers, but there's an immense amount of behind-the-scenes work involved. Comedians don't simply go play sold-out stadiums by telling jokes off the top of their heads. They go to dozens of smaller comedy clubs to work on their material before appearing in front of a large audience. They change their inflection or a specific word to test the responses from the audience until they've perfected the end joke.

Before doing a nine-minute monologue when he hosted *Saturday Night Live*, Aziz Ansari said he probably did more than 100 stand-up sets over a month-long period to get it exactly how he wanted it. Chris Rock, another comedian who spends an inordinate amount of time honing his routines, became Ansari's mentor. Here's what Rock had to say about his protege's preparation for *SNL* in an interview:

Yeah, he knew he had to do it 100 times. Anybody that's really good over-prepares, and he's got no problem. He kind of embraces it. You go to the Comedy Cellar any night and Aziz is in the booth and he's got his headphones on and he's listening to his set from the night before. He's not listening to the new Kendrick. [Laughs.] He's going over his set.

When you watch these comedians perform, it looks effortless – like they were simply born with it. People who make it look easy undoubtedly have God-given talent, but more often than not, it's their dedication and countless hours of practice that make the final result appear so natural.

Just as great performers prepare exhaustively to make their work look natural, investors succeed by creating a plan in advance that allows them to stay disciplined – often by resisting the urge to act. The good news when it comes to investing is you don't necessarily need to be the hardest worker to succeed. You just have to put in some preparation ahead of time.

Doing nothing is a decision

Researchers in Israel studied nearly 300 penalty kicks from professional soccer leagues and championship matches to gain a general sense of the strategy for both goalies and strikers. For the uninitiated, each side gets five shots on goal in a sudden-death soccer match if it's still tied after extra time. Whoever scores the most goals wins. Goalkeepers are at a severe disadvantage due to the sheer size of the goal. The striker has a clear advantage, so they score a goal in roughly four out of five opportunities, on average.

The study discovered the goalkeeper would dive left or right nearly 94% of the time, meaning the other 6% of the time they stayed in the middle hoping the kick would come right down the pipe. But what about the strikers? As you can see from the distribution of kicks in Figure 2.1, the strikers kicked it dead center far more often than the goalies stayed put.

Figure 2.1: Penalty kicks – strikers versus goalies

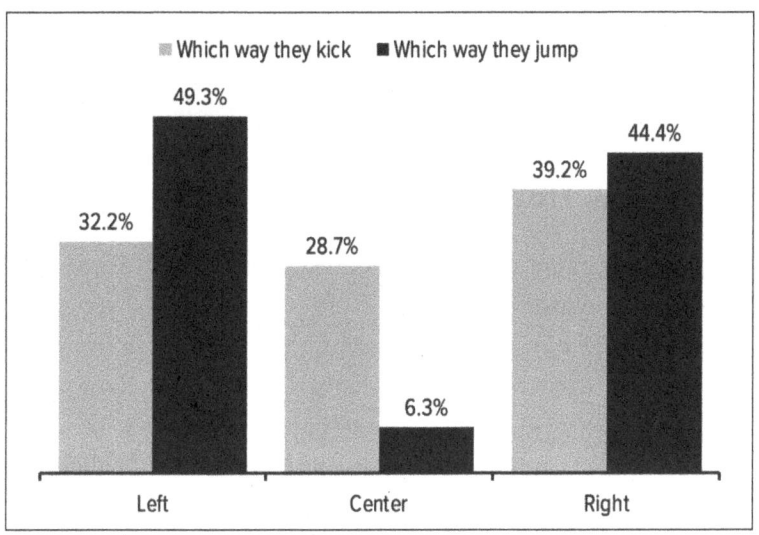

Source: Bar-Eli, Azar, Ritov, Keidar-Levin, and Schein.

The distribution of kicks was fairly even across the left, center, and right sides of the goal. However, goalkeepers disproportionately dove to the left or right when attempting to make saves. Those are the highlight plays you see on SportsCenter and social media.

In fact, the ball strikers were five times more likely to kick it down the middle than goalies were to stay in the center. This imbalance led researchers to investigate whether goalkeepers could improve their save rate by guarding the middle more often. Their findings suggested that save percentages could nearly double if goalkeepers distributed their save positioning more evenly among left, right, and center positions.

When shown the results of the research, goalies told the academics to kick rocks. Many goalies admitted they would feel a greater sense of regret staying in the middle and conceding a goal to the sides than if they dove and missed. Diving shows effort. At least they tried. Standing still and watching the ball simply wasn't an option because they don't want to look like a fool.

This study offers a fascinating look into human psychology – our innate bias toward action over inaction. Taking action provides a sense of control, even if that control is merely an illusion.

That illusion of control applies to investing as well.

How to win at investing

In many areas of life, effort correlates with results – study harder, and your grades improve; practice more, and you get better at sports; hit the gym consistently, and you can transform your body. Unfortunately, this principle doesn't apply to investing. There are no extra points awarded for degree of difficulty in your portfolio. Ironically, the harder you try, the worse your results tend to be. More action often leads to unnecessary and avoidable mistakes.

In his classic investment book, *Winning the Loser's Game*, legendary investment thinker Charles Ellis lays out three different ways you can win the game of investing:

1. **The first way is physically exhausting**. You outwork the competition. You put in more time and energy in hopes of gaining an informational or structural edge in the markets.
2. **The second way is mentally exhausting**. You outsmart the competition. You use your brainpower and intellect to outsmart other market participants.
3. **The third way is emotionally exhausting**. You are more rational than the competition. You have an unemotional long-term process you follow come hell or high water.

The problem with option one is there is little evidence of a high correlation between trying harder and investment performance. More activity doesn't necessarily make you better at investing. Warren Buffett once said, "The stock market is designed to transfer money from the active to the patient."

The problem with option two is that there will always be people who are smarter than you. Millions of MBAs, CFAs, PhDs, and literal rocket scientists are trying their hand at beating the market. They have better technology, data and researchers than you do. Luckily, surviving in the markets doesn't necessarily require you to have the highest IQ to win. Buffett also said, "Investing is not a game where the guy with the 160 IQ beats the guy with the 130 IQ. Once you have ordinary intelligence, what you need is the temperament to control the urges that get other people into trouble in investing."

Temperament brings us to the most realistic option for most investors – the emotionally exhausting approach, option three. An emotionally exhausting investment approach does present its own set of challenges. You have to be willing to look past short-term outcomes when following a long-term approach. You have to be willing to live with volatility and losses at times. It's also boring and not as sexy to take a longer-term stance in the markets. And maybe the hardest part of all is that it's much easier to do something rather than nothing, even when doing nothing is the right move.

In the information age, the bias towards action will only increase in the future. It's never been easier to pay attention to every headline. Social media glorifies day traders and people who get rich overnight. Patience is a virtue no one has time for anymore. The only way you can do nothing is by performing all of the heavy lifting up front. You need a durable investment plan that you can stick with through a wide range of market and economic environments.

Vanguard's Jack Bogle liked to say, "Don't just do something. Stand there!" In other words, stay the course.* Staying the course means going against your own emotions at times. Staying the course means thinking and acting for the long term even when it doesn't feel right in the short term. Staying the course means preparing not predicting. Staying the course means doing nothing when that's what your plan

---

* *Stay the Course* was the title of Bogle's final book before he passed away.

calls for. Unfortunately, doing nothing is hard work because markets constantly tempt you into changing your portfolio.

One of the best ways to stay the course is by automating good decisions in advance. You can use technology to create guidelines that will automatically buy, sell, or change your asset allocation using pre-established rules. You can automate your contributions, dividend reinvestment, portfolio rebalance and buy/sell rules. Making those decisions ahead of time helps you avoid many of the most common investor mistakes, which are typically made in the heat of the moment.

Investing is hard. You're forced to deal with constant uncertainty, volatility, fear, greed, and an endless stream of noise. Your worst enemy in the markets is not the person on the other side of the trade – it's you.

Doing more, trying harder, making more trades and paying more attention to your portfolio can be hazardous to your wealth. The most important work you can do as an investor is proper preparation. And when it is time to act, it will be because your plan tells you to, not because of some scary headlines or talking head on financial television forcing your hand.

Making it look easy requires plenty of hard work.

Next up, a chapter about the silent killer of your finances.

3.
THE GREAT INFLATION

"A nickel ain't worth a dime anymore."

—YOGI BERRA

INFLATION IS A relatively new phenomenon.

In modern economic times, prices didn't start rising on a sustained basis until the 1940s. From 1800 to 1940, prices rose at an average inflation rate of just 0.2% per year, meaning the cost of living was just 28% higher in 1940 than it was at the onset of the 19th century. There were nearly 70 separate periods of deflation, where prices fell.

The worst bout of deflation followed the Panic of 1873, also called the Long Depression, which saw prices fall 40% over the next two-plus decades.*

There were, of course, bouts of inflation in that time. It's just that the deflationary busts balanced out the inflationary booms. That all changed following the Second World War. Before the 1940s, the biggest catalyst that drove U.S. economic cycles was war, mainly

---

* Prices falling 40% sounds like a screaming deal until you realize that deflation was accompanied by two decades of economic stagnation. Inflation itself isn't necessarily good, but it's the lesser of two evils when compared to deflation. Deflation means lower wage growth and a shrinking economy.

because there were so many of them. From the War of 1812 to the Civil War to the First World War, the economic cycle followed a fairly predictable pattern.

A Federal Reserve research paper from the 1940s outlined the four phases of post-war economies in the United States:

1. **A period of uncertainty**. This phase involved some turmoil and confusion because the country moved from wartime spending and production to a more normal peacetime economy.
2. **A post-war recovery**. This phase involved speculation, an inflationary spike and overheating from post-war excesses which would eventually lead to a slowdown.
3. **A post-war depression**. The deflationary busts following the post-war booms were brutal once government spending slowed. There were 13-year periods of deflation and stagnation following the War of 1812, the Civil War and the First World War, respectively.
4. **Prosperity**. This was the back-to-normal phase where companies were all producing and selling goods as they were before the war and the economy got back on track.

The Second World War permanently disrupted this cycle. Although there was a significant post-war recovery in the late 1940s, it was not followed by a deflationary bust. Inflation surged during the initial boom, reaching as high as 19% in the years after the war, but then stabilized at a more moderate level without triggering a depression. The 1950s experienced substantial growth in the middle class as soldiers who returned from the war sought to build their lives in the suburbs, start families, buy homes, and spend some money.

Inflation has been on a new course ever since.

Recall that inflation from 1800 to 1940 was less than 30% in total. Then from 1941 to 2024, prices in the United States rose 3.8% annually on average, or more than 2,200% in total. From 1941 to 1967, inflation averaged 3.3% per year in the U.S. That was much higher than previous cycles, but reasonable given the fact there were no more depressions and the economy was growing like crazy.

Then the train left the tracks.

A combination of factors – including excessive government spending, the Vietnam War, supply chain issues and oil price shocks – contributed to unprecedented inflation in the 1970s. Inflation started getting out of control in the late 1960s and would go on a tear through the early 1980s. From 1968 to 1981, the inflation rate in the U.S. averaged 7.5% per year. It ended a year with double-digit inflation three times – in 1974, 1979 and 1980 – over this 14-year period. There wasn't a single year in the entire decade of the 1970s when inflation came in below 3%. In eight out of the 10 years, the annual inflation rate was above 5%.

The 1950s and parts of the 1960s were boom times for investors. But the 1970s was a Mad Max hellscape. U.S. stock market performance was subpar in the 1970s, but not as bad as you'd think, at least on a nominal basis. The S&P 500 returned nearly 6% per year for the decade. Not bad, right? The problem is that the annual inflation rate was 7.4% in the 1970s, meaning stocks had negative *real* returns. The S&P 500 lost more than 26% of its value from 1970 to 1979 on an inflation-adjusted basis. On a real basis, the 1970s were about as bad as the 1930s.

As shown in Table 3.1, the 1970s is the only decade in modern economic history where cash (T-bills)* beat both stocks (S&P 500) and bonds (10-year Treasuries). In the 1970s, cash returned 6.3%, with bonds at 5.4% and stocks at 5.9%.

---

* Cash equivalents such as savings accounts, money market funds, CDs, T-bills, etc., are a good hedge against inflation because short-term interest rates tend to rise when inflation is high. The fact that cash is a short-term asset allows investors to pick up higher yields much more quickly, whereas bond investors have interest rate risk since they typically have yields locked in for longer time frames.

Table 3.1: Asset class returns by decade

Decade	Stocks	Bonds	Cash
1930s	−0.9%	4.0%	1.0%
1940s	8.5%	2.5%	0.5%
1950s	19.5%	0.8%	2.0%
1960s	7.7%	2.4%	4.0%
1970s	5.9%	5.4%	6.3%
1980s	17.3%	12.0%	8.8%
1990s	18.0%	7.4%	4.8%
2000s	−1.0%	6.3%	2.7%
2010s	13.4%	4.1%	0.6%

Source: NYU (S&P 500, 10-year Treasuries, 3-month T-bills).

The 1970s weren't just a poor decade for the stock market. Inflation wreaked havoc on the economy too, which performed dreadfully.

There was a recession to kick off the decade which lasted most of 1970. Then came the nasty downturn from late 1973 through the spring of 1975 when the unemployment rate reached nearly 9% and the stock market got cut in half. The inflation rate and unemployment finally declined following that downturn, but it didn't last. High inflation wouldn't go away. The Federal Reserve was forced to jack up interest rates into double-digit territory to tame the inflationary beast. Mortgage rates hit nearly 20% by 1982. It took two recessions in the first three years of the 1980s to finally break the back of inflation. The unemployment rate in the U.S. topped out by the end of 1982 at almost 11%. The U.S. was in a recession for one-third of this dreadful period.

Everyone hates high inflation

In December 1970, the *Time* magazine cover story showed a picture of a dollar with a tear running down George Washington's cheek. It said the dollar was worth 73 cents. By the end of the decade, one dollar in 1970 would be worth roughly 45 cents from the effects of inflation.

Gallup has surveyed Americans for 90 years, asking them about the country's most important problems. The high cost of living ranked number one on the list of worries every year from 1973 to 1981. The populace despises high inflation with the hatred of a thousand suns and people in the 1970s made this known.

They didn't just grumble about it – they protested. Truck drivers staged national strikes over gas price spikes and rationing. In Pennsylvania, one protest turned into a full-blown riot. Meanwhile, the housing market came to a screeching halt due to high mortgage rates, as few people were willing to take out loans at such exceptionally high interest rates. One homebuilder scribbled a note on a wooden block and sent it to Fed Chairman Paul Volcker, which read, "Dear Mr. Volcker, I am beginning to feel as useless as this knothole. Where will our children live?" A trade publication published a wanted poster of Volcker in 1982 accusing him and the Federal Reserve of "premeditated and cold-blooded murder of millions of small businesses."

The New York Times published a front-page story in which they interviewed regular people across the country to see how inflation was impacting their lives:

> In interviews across the country, *The New York Times* found that the 'throwaway society' of the late 1960s and early 1970s is being replaced, in many cases, by a new ethic of economy. People are driving cars longer and wearing clothes more often, planting their own gardens and fixing their own plumbing.
>
> Many Americans use the same words to describe this new attitude: 'We buy only what we need, not what we want.' But this means that some of the juice of life, from new stereos to trips to the beach, is getting squeezed dry by the pressure of rising prices.

One of those interviews was with a bread salesman named Terry McLamb from Raleigh, North Carolina. McLamb was not fond of inflation:

Terry McLamb, the bread salesman, has seen his income rise from $9,000 to $15,000 a year in five years, but says: 'I was getting along better on the lower income. It's all got to come to a point somewhere, but I don't know where.'

In the five years ending 1978, the consumer price index was up 47%. McLamb's income rose 67% in that same period. His income outstripped inflation by 20%, yet he was miserable.*

That's the insidious nature of inflation and why people hate it so much – even when you're technically earning more, rising prices can make you feel like you're falling behind. Workers see higher wages as something earned, while higher prices feel like theft.

Why is this the case?

A Purdue University professor studied weekly sales data for eggs in California to determine how the price changes impacted consumer demand. In a rational world, you would expect consumer demand to change equally whether prices go up or down. That's what they teach you in economics textbooks. If prices fall a little you would expect demand to rise a little. If prices rise a little, you would expect demand to fall a little. Economics 101.

But that's not the case in the real world. In the real world, people have emotions that aren't accounted for in economics textbooks and feelings can impact money decisions.

The researchers found that consumers do buy a little more when egg prices fall. But when egg prices rise, consumers cut back their consumption two-and-a-half times more. The fancy way of saying this is that egg prices have an asymmetric demand profile. When prices drop people buy a little more. But when prices rise, they cut way back on egg consumption.

People overreact to price gains because losses sting twice as bad as

---

* Median income in the U.S. was approximately $13,500 in 1978 when this piece was published, so Mr. McLamb's income was 15% higher than that.

gains feel good.* You could call this irrational if you'd like, but this is who we are as humans. It's in our DNA.

And that is why people hate inflation. It feels like a loss and losses are painful.

Warren Buffett explains how inflation impacts stocks

Investors are none too fond of inflation either. While the stock market is a wonderful hedge against inflation in the long term, it's not a fan of rapidly rising prices in the short term.

Let's take a look at the numbers. I calculated the returns for the S&P 500 in a given year when inflation was high, low, rising and falling from one year to the next from 1928 through 2024. The results are shown in Figure 3.1.

Figure 3.1: Stock market returns by inflation regime (1928–2024)

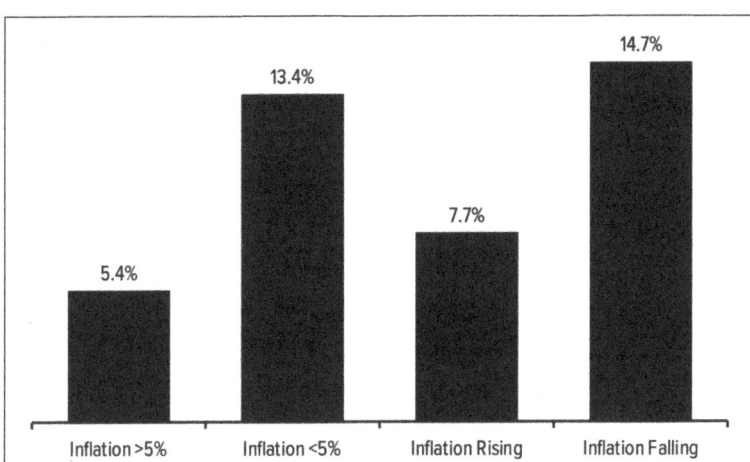

Source: Damodaran Online, Stern School of Business, NYU.

---

* Inflation brings about the same feelings of loss aversion we talk about in Chapter 4.

As a general rule of thumb, when inflation is high, average returns tend to be lower. When inflation is rising from one year to the next, average returns tend to be lower. When inflation is low, average returns tend to be higher. When inflation is falling from one year to the next, average returns tend to be higher. This is not always the case, but the stock market tends to have worse returns when inflation is high and/or rising.

Warren Buffett penned an op-ed in *Fortune* titled "How Inflation Swindles the Equity Investor" in 1977 that helps explain this phenomenon. The Oracle of Omaha's main takeaway is that stocks are more similar to bonds than most investors assume, especially when it comes to investing during a highly inflationary environment:

> The main reason, I believe, is that stocks, in economic substance, are really very similar to bonds.
>
> I know that this belief will seem eccentric to many investors. They will immediately observe that the return on a bond (the coupon) is fixed, while the return on an equity investment (the company's earnings) can vary substantially from one year to another. True enough. But anyone who examines the aggregate returns that have been earned by companies during the postwar years will discover something extraordinary: the returns on equity have in fact not varied much at all.

Buffett's reasoning here is based on the idea that the return on equity (ROE) for U.S. corporations is relatively stable over time at around 12%. ROE measures how much profit corporations generate for every $1 of shareholder equity. Obviously, the prices people are willing to pay for that ROE can vary quite violently at times, but the ROE itself is relatively stable.

Using this framework, you can think of stocks as something of a perpetual bond that never comes due. If the ROE on stocks doesn't change all that much, higher inflation would be harmful since investors would be receiving a lower share of profits after accounting for a higher cost of living.

Buffett explains:

> Even if you agree that the 12% equity coupon is more or less immutable, you still may hope to do well with it in the years ahead. It's conceivable that you will. After all, a lot of investors did well with it for a long time. But your future results will be governed by three variables: the relationship between book value and market value, the tax rate, and the inflation rate.
>
> So there we are: 12% before taxes and inflation; 7% after taxes and before inflation; and maybe 0% after taxes and inflation. It hardly sounds like a formula that will keep all those cattle stampeding on TV.
>
> As a common stockholder you will have more dollars, but you may have no more purchasing power.

Unfortunately, this means high inflation can be bad for both stocks and bonds.*

From 1950 through the end of 1981, long-term U.S. government bonds were up 2.1% per year. That's not a great annual return, but it's not terrible considering interest rates went from around 2% in the early 1950s to more than 15% by the early 1980s. Higher rates hurt initially, but they helped eventually as better yields lead to higher income payments. But those income payments come in the form of nominal dollars that don't change. After inflation, long bonds lost nearly 60% of their value from 1950 to 1981. Inflation massacred fixed income along with household budgets and the economy.

The story of inflation is not merely about numbers or percentages;

---

* Many investors assume the biggest risk when investing in bonds is interest rates. Since bond prices and interest rates are inversely related, bond prices fall when rates go up. While that is true, the biggest risk to high-quality bonds over the long term is inflation eating away at your periodic income payments which are worth less and less on a real basis as inflation rises.

it's about people – household budgets squeezed by rising prices, investors navigating volatile markets, and policymakers grappling with tough choices. The lesson to be learned from the Great Inflation of the 1970s is that rapidly rising prices have a huge impact on consumer psychology, household budgets, government policy, and your portfolio. One of the main reasons to invest for the long run is because inflation erodes your purchasing power. But you can beat the silent killer with a good job, a good mortgage, and ownership in good businesses through the stock market.

In the next chapter, we'll look at the three best ways to hedge against inflation.

4:

THE THREE
BEST INFLATION
HEDGES

"People who buy things are suckers."

—RON SWANSON

A MILLION DOLLARS IS a lot of money. Households worth $1 million or more make up just 1.5% of the world's population.*

The Millionaire Next Door by Thomas Stanley and William Danko was originally published in 1996. It belongs on the Mount Rushmore of personal finance books because it broke new ground on how most Americans become millionaires. Most millionaires aren't flashy spenders, but rather people who live below their means and save diligently. True wealth is the spending you don't see. These millionaires next door accumulated their riches by prioritizing hard work, discipline, long-term investing and solid financial habits that compound over many years into a two-comma net worth.

However, a million dollars doesn't go nearly as far as it used to. One

---

* Millionaires make up 1.5% of the population, yet they control nearly half of the world's wealth. In America, millionaire households (including home equity) make up 18% of the population.

million dollars in 1996 was worth just $475,000 by the end of 2024. Said another way, it would take more than $2 million in 2024 to be on equal footing with $1 million in 1996 in terms of spending power. A 3% inflation rate cuts the value of a dollar in half in 23 years. At 4%, inflation cuts your money in half in 17 years.

You can complain all you want about this, but it's not going away as long as the economy keeps growing and workers demand higher wages. You just have to be intelligent about how to hedge the inflationary beast.

Let's look at the three best ways for investors to combat inflation.

The three best inflation hedges

The three best hedges against inflation for most people are a good job, home ownership and stocks for the long run. Let's review each of these in turn.

1. A good job

The inflation rate can be helpful for understanding trends in the overall economy, but it's an imperfect measure for your specific household. You are not the aggregate inflation rate. Your household inflation rate is personal. It depends on where you live, how you live, how much you spend, what you spend your money on and, most importantly, your job. Wage growth is personal too because people's income trajectory does not necessarily match the averages.

The ability to grow your income in the face of rising prices is your best hedge against inflation. The best career advice I've ever received is to become indispensable to whoever you're working for. Easier said than done, but that helps ensure you're paid a fair wage and have the ability to negotiate a higher salary over time. One of the best ways to improve your career prospects is to become a lifelong learner.

When asked for a piece of career advice at a conference, Nvidia's Jensen Huang replied, "Dedicate yourself to learning all the time, doing the best possible work you can, and leave everything on the field. I'm not at all ambitious. I don't aspire to do more. I aspire to do better at what I'm currently doing."

As Steve Martin once said, "Be so good they can't ignore you."

Most personal finance experts focus on saving, investing and frugality. You can only cut so much from your budget. The way to really get ahead is to invest in yourself and improve your earning power. The more you make the more you can save and invest.

2. A home with a fixed-rate mortgage

When inflation rears its ugly head, consumers focus on the price of eggs, gas and bacon going up, but the two biggest spending categories for households by far are housing and transportation. This is illustrated in Figure 4.1.

Figure 4.1: How Americans spend their money

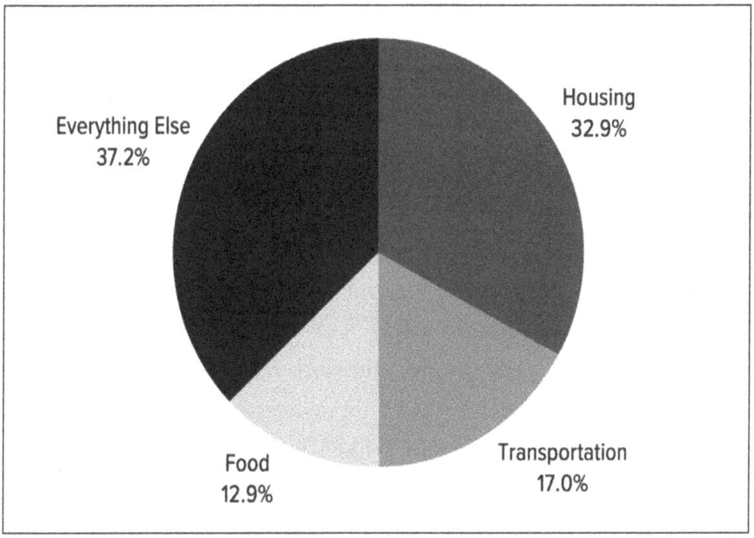

Source: BLS.

Housing and transportation make up half of all household consumption. Get them right from a budgeting perspective and your financial life becomes much easier. Overspend on these two areas and it becomes much harder to get ahead financially. This is why a fixed-rate mortgage can be so beneficial if you choose the right house and have the ability to service the debt.

You should earn more money as you progress in your career. That makes fixed payments easier to stomach from a budgeting perspective over time. You can also write off the interest you pay on the loan as a deduction for tax purposes in the U.S. Plus, inflation eats into the value of your payment slowly but surely over time. Housing prices also tend to rise when inflation moves higher. Owning a home is a wonderful hedge against inflation.

Let's do a deep dive into why that is the case.

A short history of fixed-rate mortgages

The 30-year fixed-rate mortgage is one of the greatest consumer financial products ever created. It happened almost by accident. The fixed-rate mortgage originated as a result of the Great Depression. Before that economic avalanche reshaped the United States, homeowners typically took out mortgage loans with terms of three to five years. At the end of the loan term, borrowers would either pay off the remaining balance in a large lump sum, or refinance into a new loan with similar terms. Down payments were significantly higher too, at around 50% of the home's value.

The economic devastation of the 1930s made it nearly impossible for homeowners to keep up with their mortgage payments. By 1933, over 40% of mortgages were in default. Foreclosure, which was once considered a shameful last resort, lost its stigma during the Great Depression as homeowners stopped paying their mortgages in large numbers. Franklin Delano Roosevelt's New Deal reshaped how banks and homeowners alike approached the home-buying process to help lower the strain on the financial system. Loans were extended to 15-year terms and eventually pushed out ever further to 20-, 25- and finally 30-year increments to make it easier for borrowers to make their monthly payments. Mortgage loans now comprise more than 70% of all consumer debt in the United States. By the mid-2020s, almost 95% of all mortgages outstanding in the United States had a fixed rate.*

Most homeowners in the United States put down anywhere from 5–20% and finance the rest. Sure, you have to pay interest on that loan, but the payment never changes if you choose a fixed rate for 30 years. Every single month, you pay the principal and the interest on the loan and the total never changes.** To paraphrase Wooderson – Matthew McConaughey's breakout role – from *Dazed and Confused*, "That's what I love about these fixed-rate mortgages, man, I make more money, the payment stays the same."

The Great Depression changed the way households finance the biggest purchase of their lives but it wasn't until the Great Inflation of the 1970s that housing turned into the American Dream in a big way.

The American Dream

Investors had it tough in the 1970s. Stocks were dead money. Bonds got crushed by inflation and rising interest rates. You could earn money in cash-like investments, but that's not very exciting to talk about at cocktail parties. So investors were forced into the loving arms of housing as both an investment and inflation hedge.

Joe Nocera explains in his book, *A Piece of the Action*:

---

* This is not the case in most other developed nations. In Australia, more than 80% of mortgages have variable rates, meaning they can change when market rates change. In Canada, Sweden, Norway, Portugal, Finland and Japan, more than half of all mortgages are on an adjustable rate. This is a good thing when interest rates fall, but not so great when they rise, which tends to occur when inflation rises.

** There are, of course, ancillary costs to homeownership such as property taxes, insurance, maintenance and upkeep that can and will change over time. Owning a home is not a free lunch.

Among those who already owned a home, the talk had an awed, slightly obsessive, even giddy quality; among those who didn't, it had an awed, slightly embittered, and frankly envious quality. A house wasn't just part of the American dream anymore; it was part of the money revolution. And that was sad.

In 1979, an economist for Paine Webber pleaded for Americans to buy a home, writing in *The New York Times*, "'Never buy what you can't afford' was the admonition of our parents. Today, the statement has been changed to, 'You can't afford not to buy it.'"

Once upon a time, the American Dream was not just to own your own home but to own it outright by paying off your mortgage. That vision began to fade in the 1970s because of soaring inflation. Paying off a mortgage wasn't practical when inflation took huge bites out of your debt payments. Why pay it off early if waiting made each successive payment worth less and less on a real basis? A house went from being a roof over your head to the biggest financial asset for most families and the simplest way to hedge sky-high inflation. This shift happened largely because housing was one of the few assets that appreciated in the 1970s.

Housing prices nationwide were up nearly 130% in the 1970s, good enough for annual returns of almost 9% per year. Housing was one of the only asset classes that actually beat inflation (see Figure 4.2).*

---

* Gold was the other big winner of the 1970s, rising nearly 30% per year after Nixon took the U.S. off the gold standard for good. Unfortunately there was no gold ETF back then, meaning you actually had to buy gold bars or coins to take advantage.

Figure 4.2: Asset class returns (1970s)

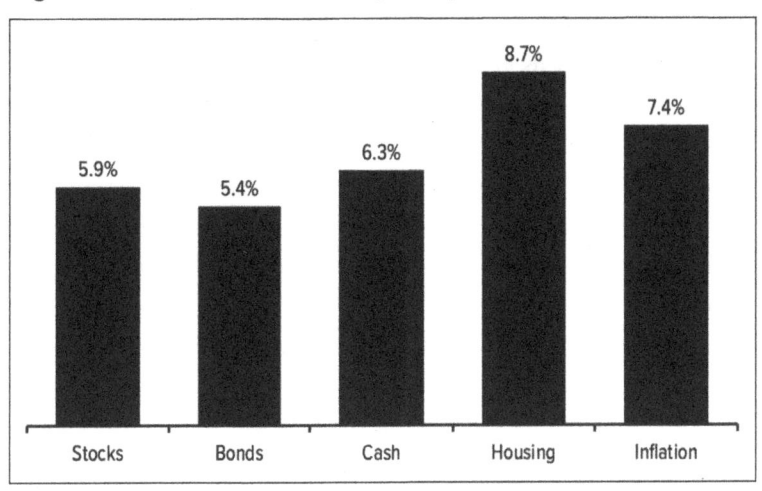

Source: NYU.

This begs the question: How did housing protect homeowners when the other main asset classes faltered?

Think about it this way – let's say the inflation rate averages 3% per year over the next 30 years. If you stash your savings under your mattress for the entirety of that time frame, by the end of three decades, every dollar you started with would be worth just 40 cents. This is why you want to invest your cash instead of just sitting on it.

A fixed-rate mortgage works like that but in reverse. Let's say you take out a $400,000 loan at 6% using a 30-year fixed-rate mortgage. Your payment would be roughly $2,400 a month (not including things like property taxes and home insurance). Your $2,400 monthly payment stays the same for the life of the loan. But the nominal dollars you use to repay that loan will be worth less and less in the future because of inflation.

Plus, wages rise when prices rise, making it more expensive to hire construction workers. The cost of building materials goes up. Commodity prices increase. All of these factors make it more costly to build new homes which, in effect, makes existing homes worth even more from a replacement cost perspective. Inflation causes housing prices to rise and eats away at your debt.

Robert Shiller assembled a database of U.S. home prices going back to 1890. The inflation-adjusted return for housing nationwide from 1890 through 2024 was around 0.6% per year. If we measure from 1970, it's a 1% real return. This doesn't sound all that great compared to the stock market, which has real returns of 5–7% depending on the lookback period.

However, it's worth mentioning that calculating the return on the roof over your head is nearly impossible. You have to include the ancillary costs (insurance, property taxes, upkeep, etc.), the leverage involved and the imputed rent because you have to live somewhere whether you own or rent. I'd venture to guess there isn't a single homeowner alive who knows what the actual dollar-for-dollar return is on their home. And that's OK! Owning a home is not like buying and holding a stock. You can't live in your Apple or Microsoft or index fund shares.

However, even if we take Shiller's numbers at face value, earning a return only slightly above the rate of inflation over the long term on a building you and your family are happily living in is a wonderful deal.

3. Stocks for the long run

The stock market can struggle with an inflationary spike in the short term, but stocks for the long run are still your best investment hedge against the corrosive effects of inflation.

The U.S. stock market has beaten the inflation rate by nearly 7% per year over the long haul. One of the reasons for this is the fact that corporations grow their earnings and dividends at a healthy clip above inflation. Dividends have grown more than two percentage points faster than the annual inflation rate over the long haul. Inflation-adjusted earnings growth has come in at around 3% per year over the past 100 years or so.

And while real returns can suffer during higher periods of inflation, you hedge against those times when inflation is running low. Take a look at the cycles of real returns over the years in Table 4.1.

Table 4.1: Stock market cycles

Time Frame	Nominal Returns	Inflation	Annual Real Returns
1928-1942	0.7%	−0.2%	0.9%
1943-1965	15.4%	2.8%	12.6%
1966-1981	6.0%	7.0%	−1.0%
1982-1999	18.3%	3.3%	15.0%
2000-2008	−3.6%	2.5%	−6.1%
2009-2024	14.5%	2.6%	11.9%

Sources: NYU (S&P 500); FRED.

The data shows that inflation spiked in the 1970s, leaving investors with decent nominal returns but awful real returns. Investors in the U.S. stock market lost more than 35% after adjusting for inflation from 1966 to 1981. The 1980s and 1990s still experienced some inflation, but it was falling and that led to glorious returns for investors. The 2000 to 2008 time frame was bookended by two gargantuan crashes of more than 50%. When you take into account the 3% inflation, investors lost more than 6% per year for nearly a decade. Ouch.

Some claim that periods like 1966 to 1981 show why the stock market isn't always your best bet. But it's because of periods like this that you have to stay invested. Yes, returns from 1966 to 1981 were negative on a real basis. But let's combine that inflationary bust with the booms that preceded and followed it.

From 1943 to 1981, nominal annual returns were 11.4%. With a 4.5% annual inflation rate, real returns were roughly 7% per year over the entire period. From 1966 to 1999, nominal annual returns were 12.3% against a 5% annual inflation rate, leaving investors with 7.3% real returns over 34 years. The same applies when we combine other down cycles with up cycles. From 1982 to 2008, real returns were 7.3% per year. The boom of the 1980s and 1990s smoothed out the bust from 2000 to 2008.

The best way to prepare for terrible periods in the stock market is by staying invested during the glorious times. The best way to offset periods of low real returns is by staying invested during periods of high real returns. There's only one guaranteed way to lose money to inflation – don't invest your savings at all.

Some of you might be thinking: No thanks, I'll just invest in stocks when returns are high and sit on the sidelines when returns are low.

Good luck with that. In the next chapter, we'll look at the folly of trying to time these market cycles.

5.

TIMING THE
MARKET

"Timing the market is a fool's game,
whereas time in the market is your
greatest natural advantage."

—NICK MURRAY

IN OCTOBER 2008, Warren Buffett penned an op-ed for *The New York Times* with a simple headline that read:

Buy American. I Am.

He explained:

The financial world is a mess, both in the United States and abroad. Its problems, moreover, have been leaking into the general economy, and the leaks are now turning into a gusher. In the near term, unemployment will rise, business activity will falter and headlines will continue to be scary.

So... I've been buying American stocks.

Buffett was taking his own advice about being greedy when others were fearful. And boy was everyone fearful.

The financial system was on the verge of collapse. Lehman Brothers, which had been operating for nearly 160 years, went out of business in September. The U.S. government nationalized the federal mortgage insurers Freddie Mac and Fannie Mae. The Fed was forced to bail out AIG while the Treasury injected $700 billion to bail out the country's biggest banks. Banks were going under left and right. Stocks were crashing. Our pets' heads were falling off! It was a bloodbath.

When Buffett wrote his op-ed, the S&P 500 had already cratered by over 40%. Investors hoped the legendary investor's calm words would stop the bleeding. Buying when there is blood in the streets tends to work out over the long term, but there was much more blood to be spilled during this crisis.

From the day Buffett's piece was published through the eventual bottom a few months later, the stock market shed a further one-third of its value. That means investors experienced a 40% crash through the fall of 2008 followed by an additional 33% shellacking from there until the market finally found a bottom. All told, the S&P 500 was down nearly 60% from the peak in October of 2007 through the bottom in early March of 2009.

Of course, Buffett admitted even he couldn't time the market perfectly (emphasis is mine):

> Let me be clear on one point: **I can't predict the short-term movements of the stock market.** I haven't the faintest idea as to whether stocks will be higher or lower a month or a year from now. What is likely, however, is that the market will move higher, perhaps substantially so, well before either sentiment or the economy turns up. So if you wait for the robins, spring will be over.

Buffett was buying individual stocks at the time, but let's say you heeded his advice by buying an S&P 500 index fund on October 16,

2008. Yes, you would have almost immediately gone through a 30%+ crash over the next five months. But had you held on for the long term, that crash would become a distant memory.

From the time Buffett bought America through the end of 2024, the S&P 500 was up a staggering 750%, good enough for an annualized return of more than 14% per year.

Short-term pain for long-term gain.

Things might not work out so wonderfully every time stocks go down in the future. Like Mr. Buffett, you or I cannot predict what will happen next in the stock market. The good news is you don't have to pinpoint the exact bottom of a bear market to make out like a bandit. As long as you can keep a long enough time horizon, even large losses in the stock market tend to be swamped by the eventual gains.

Hindsight bias

In 1966, Buffett was still running an investment partnership, managing money for some friends, family and business associates. That was a rough year for the stock market, which took a nosedive right out of the gates. After the Dow entered correction territory, a few investors in Buffett's partnership felt the need to inform him what would happen next. They warned that the stock market likely had further to fall.

Buffett gave his written response in an investor letter in May 1966:

(1) If they knew in February that the Dow was going to 865 in May, why didn't they let me in on it then; and,
(2) If they didn't know what was going to happen during the ensuing three months back in February, how do they know in May?

Buffett's investors wanted him to wait until the coast was clear. He explained his thinking on short-run market moves like this:

There is also a voice or two after any hundred point or so decline suggesting we sell and wait until the future is clearer. Let me again suggest two points: (1) the future has never been clear to me (give us a call when the next few months are obvious to you – or, for that matter the next few hours); and, (2) no one ever seems to call after the market has gone up one hundred points to focus my attention on how unclear everything is, even though the view back in February doesn't look so clear in retrospect.

Emotions are heightened during downturns, so it's no surprise that investors pay more attention and believe they can predict what comes next. It feels more comfortable to have your hands on the steering wheel. The reality is the market doesn't care about your feelings and the steering wheel doesn't work, no matter how hard you grip it. The market is in the driver's seat at all times.

The reason hindsight bias can be so detrimental to your investment performance is because it makes you feel like you can guess what's coming next when you look at the past. But it's never clear what the future will bring. I've heard countless investors over the years say some variation of the following:

Let's just sell everything and wait for the dust to settle.

I'll go to cash and then buy after the market crashes. Piece of cake.

But what if I put money to work in stocks and the market crashes even more?

I'm just going to wait until the market bottoms… then I'll buy.

The market doesn't give you an all-clear signal. No one rings a bell at the top. No one sounds an alarm at the bottom. The market won't hold your hand to make investing easier. John Templeton once said, "The investor who says, 'This time is different,' when in fact it's virtually a repeat of an earlier situation, has uttered among the four most costly words in the annals of investing."

The eight most costly words of market timing are, "I'll just wait until the coast is clear."

This is true of both tops and bottoms.

Tops and bottoms

Financial historian Frederick Lewis Allen wrote about the 1929 top before the Great Depression crash in his book *Since Yesterday*:

> No headlines will announce tonight that the Big Bull Market has reached its climax; for no headline writers – nor anybody else for that matter – can see into the future. The financial reporters will remark, to be sure, that bullish enthusiasm has resulted in 'another in the long series of consecutive new high records established by the share market,' but the comment will be casual. Men do not whip themselves into frenzies over the usual. None of us is aware, on September 3, 1929, that the people of the United States are crossing one of the great divides of national history. The way ahead is hidden, as always, by fog. Surely, we imagine, there is higher ground just ahead. Yet at this very moment the path under our feet is about to turn downward.

The crash would send stocks spiraling down more than 85% over the next three years (more on this crash later in the book). Tops are challenging to see on the horizon, but so are generational bottoms. Joe Nocera wrote about the end of the 1970s stagnation when the stock market finally bottomed in the early 1980s:

> On an otherwise inauspicious Friday in August – Friday the 13th, as it happens – the Dow Jones Industrial Average opened at 776.92. Up until then, all but one trading session that month had been a losing one; indeed, most trading sessions for the previous year and a half had resulted in losses. Volume was light.

The market seemed moribund. But when trading ended that day, the Dow had risen twelve points. The following Monday it rose another four points, and the day after that, the 17th of August, it closed at 831.24, for a gain – highly unusual in the early 1980s – of close to 40 points. Volume wasn't just heavy, it was history-making: More shares were traded the third week of August 1982 than had ever been traded in any five-day stretch before. By the end of the month, the Dow stood at 901.31. It had gained 125 points in 13 sessions.

That was the start of perhaps the greatest bull market in U.S. stock market history. No one saw it coming. Pinpointing tops and bottoms after they've already taken place is easy – just look at a chart to see where the market turns. These turning points are rarely obvious in the moment because you never know how far human nature will take things in the good or bad times.

The stock market can be counterintuitive. I could give you the headlines ahead of time and you still might not be able to predict what comes next. Investing looks easy in the rearview mirror, but the future is always unknown. The good news is you can be a successful investor without trying to guess what comes next. It just requires a touch of discipline and a dash of automation.

What about Bob?

Remember our guy Bob, the world's worst market timer, from the Introduction? I updated Bob's numbers through 2024 to see how things would have looked given some more recent downturns. This time I assumed Bob began his investment journey in 1983 and retired at age 65 at the end of 2024. Using the same assumptions from before,* this time I used five different purchases at stock market peaks:

---

* Bob kept all of his savings in a checking account until he could work up the nerve to invest in the U.S. stock market and never sold out of those initial poorly timed investments. Just like before.

- 1987 just before the worst single day in history (-20%) when stocks fell more than 30% in a week.
- The end of 1999 right before the dot-com bubble burst, cutting the stock market in half.
- The fall of 2007 just before the Great Financial Crisis caused the stock market to drop nearly 60%.
- In February of 2020 before the onset of the Covid pandemic saw stocks fall 34% in a little over a month.
- In January of 2022 as the stock market was about to drop more than 25% from the pandemic-induced inflationary spike.

Not great, Bob. Every purchase came right at a market peak before a major decline. Figure 5.1 shows the peak-to-trough declines from the points at which Bob made his purchases.

Figure 5.1: World's worst market timer

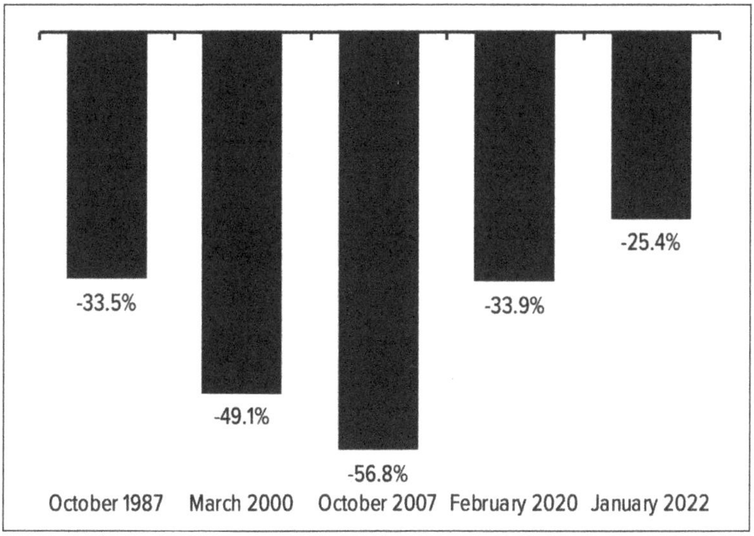

Source: YCharts.com.

Bob saved more than $200,000 in total, but ended up with nearly $1.1 million by the time he retired at 65 in 2024 because he never sold out of the stock market. That's pretty good considering he picked the five worst entry points over the course of his investing lifecycle. Even poorly timed purchases in the stock market can work out if you have a long enough time horizon.

However, Bob could have done much better by taking market timing out of the equation. What if Bob kept things simple and instead of trying to time the market by sitting in cash and waiting, he invested on a regular basis? Most normal people dollar cost average into the market by saving periodically from their paychecks, so let's assume Bob did that.

Let's say that Bob decided to invest his money on a monthly basis instead of trying to time the market. These are the amounts Bob would have saved per month over his saving and investing lifecycle:*

- 1983–1992: $167/month
- 1993–2002: $333/month
- 2003–2012: $500/month
- 2013–2022: $667/month
- 2023–2024: $833/month

With a dollar-cost averaging strategy where Bob dutifully invested his money each and every month, held onto his investments for the long haul and went on living his life, he would have entered retirement at age 65 heading into 2025 with nearly **$2.3 million**. That's a much better result with very little effort on Bob's part – he doesn't need to monitor the market or choose his entry points, he just automatically invests consistently every month.

Now let's consider the opposite of Bob's terrible market timing purchases. What if instead of investing at the top right before a giant

---

* Recall that Bob saved $2,000/year for the first 10 years of investing and increases that amount by $2,000/year every 10 years.

market crash, Bob invested towards the bottom after those crashes had already occurred? Let's transform Bob from the world's *worst* market timer into the best.

Using the same original assumptions where Bob built up his cash on the sidelines, what if instead of investing at the top of the market he invested closer to the market bottoms? This market timing strategy yielded better results than the bad market timing, with an ending balance of $1.7 million, but that's still far less than the dollar cost averaging strategy. Plus, to get this result Bob had to precisely time the bottom of those bear markets, something that no one can do with consistency.

The siren song of market timing is ever tempting, but not worth the heartache and anxiety. Jumping in and out of the market to wait for a pullback is like a gateway drug to a cash addiction. You have to be right twice – when you buy and when you sell. Pulling the trigger on a sale during a down-trending market is easy. *Just get me out at any price!* But then you have to figure out when to get back in. That's psychological warfare.

I've spoken with hundreds of investors over the years who sold out of their stocks during the 2008 financial crisis. Years later, while a new bull market was already well underway, they were still sitting in cash. They were always an emotional train wreck because they didn't know whether to wait for another crash or rip the Band-Aid off and get back in.

Market timing is an impossible long-term strategy. Warren Buffett can't do it. You can't do it. I can't do it. The only people who can do it on a consistent basis are either lucky or lying. You're better off buying stocks on a regular basis, creating an asset allocation you can stick with and keeping your emotions in check.

In the next chapter we'll take a look at the most important concept in all of finance to show why investors are so tempted to time the market and what you can do about it.

6.

THE MOST IMPORTANT CONCEPT IN INVESTING

"You lose money fast in the stock
market. You can't make it fast."

−PETER LYNCH

ANDRE AGASSI IS one of the most decorated professional tennis players of his era.

Agassi won eight Grand Slam tournaments, an Olympic gold medal and was the number-one-rated player in the world for more than 100 weeks throughout his illustrious career.

It didn't always come easy. After turning pro as a teenage prodigy, Agassi burst onto the professional tennis scene but couldn't win the big one. He reached three Grand Slam finals in 1990 and 1991, but came up short each time. Sportswriters began calling Agassi a fraud and a choke artist. That all changed when he finally broke through and won his first Grand Slam title at Wimbledon in 1992.

Winning, however, didn't change how he felt about past losses. Agassi shared the following in his excellent biography:

> But I don't feel that Wimbledon has changed me. I feel, in fact, as if I've been let in on a dirty little secret: winning changes nothing. Now that I've won a slam, I know something that very few people on earth are permitted to know. A win doesn't feel as good as a loss feels bad, and the good feeling doesn't last as long as the bad. Not even close.

This dirty little secret is true in sports and many other facets of life – losing hurts more than winning feels good. Everyone knows this feeling. You remember the pain of your favorite team's close losses more acutely than the pleasure of their wins. It's human nature.

Nobel-prize-winning behavioral psychologist Daniel Kahneman came up with the name for this inherent human condition – **loss aversion**. Over the years, Kahneman posed a simple question to various groups: If you lost $100 for incorrectly calling a coin toss, how much would you need to win on a correct call in order to take that bet? Most people settled on $200, suggesting that losing stings twice as bad as winning feels good.

This is why losing money in the markets causes so much strain on your emotions. You panic when you see your portfolio going down in value. Losses change your perception of risk. Losses are so painful you can relive them in your sleep.

Losses often lead to poor investment decisions because they activate the part of your brain that's responsible for the fight-or-flight response. Imagine someone suddenly jumping out at you from behind a bush, or coming across a spider or snake in the wild – you instinctively jump, your heart races, and adrenaline kicks in. This reaction is hardwired into you through millions of years of evolution. Our ancestors didn't have the luxury of hesitation; when faced with a tiger on the plains, survival depended on an immediate response – run or risk being eaten.

Loss aversion has been good to us as a species, but it works against you in the markets.

This is why loss aversion is the most important money concept of all.

It doesn't matter how rich or successful you are – loss aversion impacts us all. After retiring from late-night television, David Letterman talked about what it was like to compete with other late-night hosts his whole career:

> I think there's something wrong with me. It's either a character flaw or a personality disorder. It's one or the other. I haven't heard back from the lab. Maybe life is the hard way, I don't know. When the show was great, it was never as enjoyable as the misery of the show being bad. Is that human nature?

Yes, Dave, that's human nature.

Now that we know about loss aversion, let's discuss why the stock market amplifies it for investors.

You don't live in the long term

One of the stock market's most wonderful features is that the longer your time horizon, the higher your chances of experiencing gains. This is illustrated in Figure 6.1.

Figure 6.1: Stock market loss rate by holding period (S&P 500, 1950–2024)

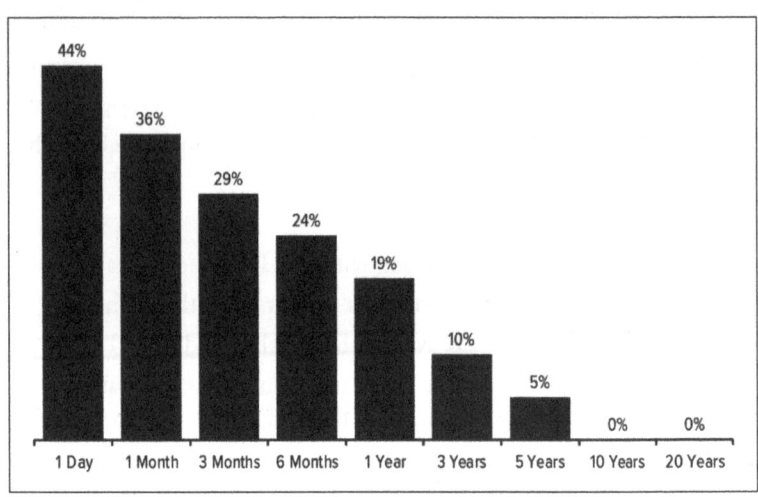

Source: YCharts.com.

As you can see, the U.S. stock market has never experienced losses over a 20-year time horizon. The historical win rate over five and 10 years is excellent as well. Even a one-year time frame has averaged gains in four out of every five years, on average, since 1950.

These percentages aren't promised going forward, but it's the trend that matters. The longer your time horizon, the more likely it is that the market will be up. You're more likely to see losses over shorter time horizons. On a monthly basis, stocks have been positive roughly two-thirds of the time. If we drill down to daily returns, now you're looking at a little better than a coin flip, with the market positive on 56% of all trading days and negative 44% of the time.

The long term gives you a higher probability of success, but ignoring the short term is impossible because you're only human. When Kahneman won the Nobel Prize for his work on human foibles, he said the following in his acceptance speech:

It is worth noting that an exclusive concern with the long term may be prescriptively sterile, because **the long term is not where life is lived**. Utility cannot be divorced from emotion, and emotion is triggered by changes. A theory of choice that completely ignores feelings such as the pain of losses and the regret of mistakes is not only descriptively unrealistic. It also leads to prescriptions that do not maximize the utility of outcomes as they are actually experienced.

Long-term returns are the only ones that matter but, as Kahneman so eloquently put it, **the long term is not where life is lived**. The long term is a series of short terms. And the short term includes 24/7 news, alerts on the tiny supercomputer in your pocket and apps that show your investment performance every second of the day. *Ignore the noise* is financial advice that sounds useful in theory but is now impossible in practice. In the information age the volume is always cranked up.

The stock market makes you feel terrible every day

Richard Thaler stood on the shoulders of Kahneman's work by taking loss aversion a step further. Thaler understood that looking at the stock market on a daily basis increases your chances of seeing a loss. The more often you look at your performance, the more likely you'll feel the down days. He coined the phrase "myopic loss aversion." Myopia is the idea that the more frequently you look at your portfolio, the more likely you are to experience the sting from loss aversion since losses are more frequent in the short run.

If you check your performance on a daily basis, the stock market will make you feel terrible every single day. Allow me to explain:

- The stock market has nearly as many down days as up days – 56% up days versus 44% down days.
- Loss aversion makes those losing days sting twice as bad as the up days feel good.
- If the gains give you one unit of pleasure while the losses give you two units of pain, when you look at your performance on a daily basis, the bad feelings will completely wipe out the good feelings and then some.

The only solution to loss aversion is extending your time horizon and not overreacting to short-run performance. If you're constantly monitoring the scoreboard for your portfolio, you'll feel the losses more often. Stop looking at your investment performance so much and you can reduce the impact of loss aversion.

How to beat loss aversion

The prescription for myopic loss aversion is to stop paying so much attention to the markets and your portfolio. That's good advice, but not effective advice in today's day and age of smartphones, social media and endless alerts.

Here are some other ways to avoid the pitfalls of loss aversion on your psyche:

Systematically take your lesser self out of the equation. Outperforming the market is hard, so your goal should be to avoid underperforming your own investments. You have to recognize your weak spots and find ways to minimize the damage when building an investment plan. Automating good decisions ahead of time helps take your lesser self out of the equation. A rules-based framework based on pre-established guidelines helps you avoid mistakes in the heat of the moment.

Filter your sources of information. My colleague Josh Brown likes to say a good financial advisor is like a bouncer who keeps the riff-raff out of the club. That same mentality should apply to your information diet. Only allow trusted sources of information behind the velvet rope for your news, analysis and opinions about the markets. The best investment decisions you make are often the things you don't invest in. The same is true of who you follow and, more importantly, avoid. The firehose of information is only harmful to those who lack a discerning filter.

The ability to ignore what others are doing with their money. One of the many unintended joys of having children is that it has forced me to avoid caring about what other people think about me as much as I did in the past. So much of my focus is on my three kids that I don't have the time or energy to care about what others think about me. It's a wonderful feeling because it frees you up from a lot of unnecessary envy, heartache and stress.

Finding contentment with your investment strategy or wealth status works in much the same way. You can't put a price on the ability to ignore what others around you are doing with their money. There will always be someone who is richer, smarter or better looking than you are. And there will always be someone making money faster than you are in the markets. Shrugging your shoulders at those situations to avoid FOMO (the fear of missing out) is a financial superpower.

Getting rich slowly. At the Sun Valley Conference a number of years ago, Jeff Bezos told a story about asking Warren Buffett for advice on a phone call. It went like this:

Bezos: "If you're the second richest guy in the world and your investment thesis is so simple why isn't everyone just copying you?"

Buffett: "Because no one wants to get rich slow."

There is no formula for getting rich in a hurry. It's pure luck or timing. But there is a formula for building wealth slowly. You have to live below your means, have a healthy savings rate, regularly invest your money into risk assets and then wait.

Waiting is the hardest part, but a combination of patience and a long time horizon will always be tough to beat in the markets.

A longer time horizon also helps reframe the pain of day-to-day losses in the stock market.

The next chapter is about the biggest losses ever seen in the U.S. stock market. Buckle up.

7.

THE WORST CRASH OF ALL TIME

"If you're not willing to react with equanimity to a market price decline of 50% two or three times a century you're not fit to be a common shareholder."

— CHARLIE MUNGER

THE FIRST HALF of the 20th century was a minefield of financial panics, war and geopolitical crises.

The Panic of 1907 nearly brought down the banking system in the United States. The financial system might have gone under if John Pierpont Morgan hadn't stepped in to save the day. The banking system was so shoddy in those days that Morgan slowed the pace of bank runs by instructing bank tellers to count out money as slowly as possible to stem the tide of withdrawals (it actually worked).

The First World War remains one of the deadliest ever fought. It's estimated 70 million military members were involved worldwide. Upwards of nine million soldiers and seven million more civilians perished in what was one of the most brutal wars on record. In 1914, the stock market closed for around four months because liquidity all but dried up once the war began.*

The war also played a major role in the spread of the Spanish Flu, which raged from 1918 to 1919. Epidemiologists today calculate somewhere in the range of 50–100 million people may have died in the worst pandemic in history. That was roughly 5% of the world's population at the time. Half of those who died were in their prime ages (20s and 30s). It lasted nearly two years, but two-thirds of the deaths took place over a 24-week period.

At the same time the pandemic spread across the globe, the United States fell into a seven-month recession that saw the economy shrink by 25%. Just 10 months after that downturn ended, the economy went into a depression. GDP contracted more than 38% in 1920, which remains the most deflationary year on record in modern economic history in the United States, with prices falling nearly 40%.

After everything that was thrown at them in this dark period, people were ready to let loose at the first glimpse of optimism. The good news came in the form of the Roaring Twenties. Inhibitions fell to the wayside as consumers experienced groundbreaking innovations that transformed their daily lives on a massive scale. The 1920s ushered in the automobile, motion pictures, the radio, the assembly line, the refrigerator, the electric razor, the washing machine, the jukebox and much more. The number of automobiles on the road tripled between 1921 and 1929. There was an unrivaled explosion of consumer spending.

After the immense pressure of the Great War, people were eager to have fun and spend money. As technological advances accelerated, consumer debt skyrocketed. By the end of the decade, an estimated one-eighth of all retail purchases were made on credit.

Borrowing was happening in the stock market too, which went parabolic in the latter half of the 1920s. Margin debt in the stock

---

* When the stock market opened back up, it took off like a rocket ship. 1915 remains the best year in the history of the Dow, which rose more than 80%.

market spiraled out of control as speculators took over, deploying an excessive amount of leverage. By 1929, nearly 20% of all listed stocks were purchased on margin. Figure 7.1 shows the Dow's run from 1915 to 1929 along with the major events that transpired.

Figure 7.1: Dow Jones Industrial Average (1915–1929 peak)

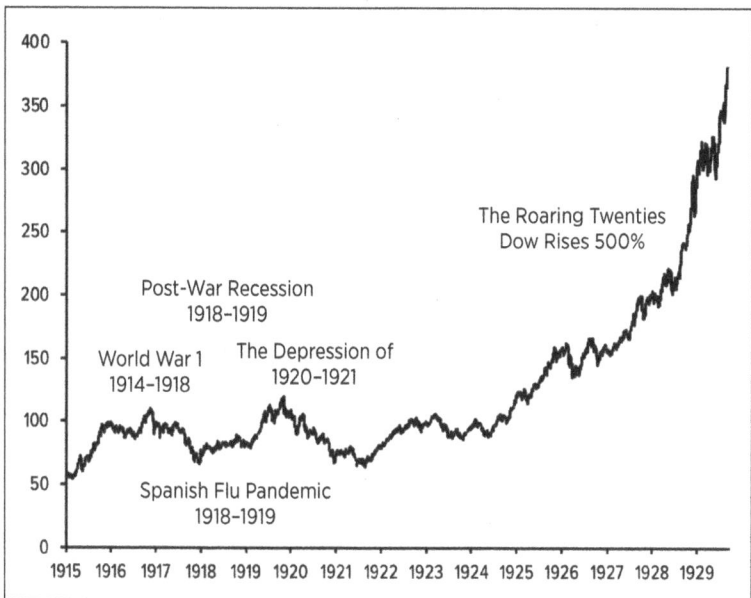

Source: YCharts.com.

In the two-year window from 1927 to 1928, the Dow Jones Industrial Average was up nearly 100% in total as the Roaring Twenties went to another level. Investor Bernard Baruch initially called the speculative rise in stock prices "madness" and claimed investors were in a state of "delirium." Baruch could only fight the bull market for so long. By 1929, he published an article that predicted lasting prosperity. The euphoria reeled him in. Most people assumed the good times would last indefinitely. Yale economist Irving Fisher infamously stated just before the stock market peaked, "Stock prices have reached what looks like a permanently high plateau." Fisher later doubled down, proclaiming, "There may be a recession in stock prices, but not anything in the nature of a crash."

It was a decade of growth and optimism the likes of which the U.S. had rarely seen. Heading into 1928, President Calvin Coolidge declared the country had entered "a new era of prosperity."

It wouldn't last.

An abrupt end to the Roaring Twenties

When it all blew up, F. Scott Fitzgerald declared, "The most expensive orgy in history is over because the utter confidence which was its essential prop received an enormous jolt, and it didn't take long for the flimsy structure to settle earthward."

There was no warning. No one rang a bell to let investors know *the* top was in. The selling began and didn't let up until a gargantuan stock market crash wiped everyone out. The Dow Jones Industrial Average reached its Roaring Twenties peak on September 3, 1929. It would decline 10% for the rest of that month. Then the real fun began.

Modern investors associate Black Monday with October 19, 1987, when the stock market suffered its worst single-day crash, dropping more than 20%. The original Black Monday took place on October 28, 1929, when the Dow dropped 13.5%, the worst day in stock market history until that point. The next day the market was down almost 12%. In just two days the stock market lost nearly one-quarter of its value. Just like that – *poof*, gone.

A few days later President Hoover tried to calm the public's mood by stating, "The fundamental business of the country is on a sound and prosperous basis." John Rockefeller, who hadn't made a public statement in decades, said he was buying the dip, "Believing that fundamental conditions of the country are sound my son and I have for some days been purchasing sound common stocks." Comedian Eddie Cantor later joked, "Sure who else has any money left?"

The answer – no one. Buyers were nonexistent. Things got so bad that there were talks of closing the market. October 1929 was one of the worst months in stock market history. Between 1929 and 1933, U.S. stocks fell by double-digits in 13 different months. Three of those months were losses of 20% or more! The worst came in September 1931, when the market lost nearly one-third of its value.

From 1926 to 2024, the U.S. stock market experienced 26 months with negative double-digit returns. Eighteen of those 26 months took place between 1929 and 1940. Volatility during the Great Crash was otherworldly. In the nine-month stretch from September 1931 through May 1932, the stock market plunged an ungodly 66%. After all of the carnage, the market finally bottomed in the summer of 1932. In a two-month window from July to August of 1932, the stock market surged more than 90%.

In two months!

This would mark the bottom. The stock market collapsed by 86% in total, by far the worst crash in U.S. stock market history. This level of loss turned $1 into 14 cents, $1,000 into $140 or $10,000 into $1,400. A $1 million portfolio would be worth $140,000 when all was said and done. It was an unfathomable loss.

You would need a gain of 615% just to break even on an 86% loss. The stock market wouldn't reach new all-time highs again on a price basis until 1954 (as shown in Figure 7.2).

Figure 7.2: Dow Jones Industrial Average (1915–1954)

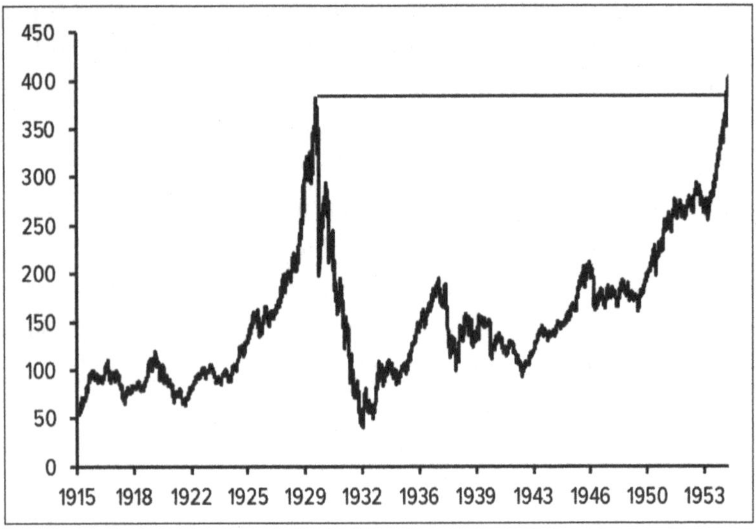

Source: YCharts.com.

Stocks for the long run *my derriere*, right?

Did the Great Crash cause the recession?

As bad as the stock market crash was in the early 1930s, the economic fallout was even worse. Fred Schwed explained it like this: "The Crash hurt people who had bought common stocks on margin; the depression hurt about everyone who was alive and some not yet born." The only silver lining to the car crash in the stock market is that most people couldn't afford to invest in stocks in the first place. It's estimated that just 2–3% of American households even owned stocks heading into the 1929 peak.

There are still debates to this day about whether the stock market crash caused the Great Depression, or vice versa.

I'll settle that debate right now – the stock market crash didn't cause the economic contraction because it was already underway by the time the market peaked in September 1929.

The economy entered a recession the month prior. From September to November of 1929, the unemployment rate in the United States rose from 750,000 to nearly three million. And that was just the beginning.

Financial historian Frederick Lewis Allen dutifully chronicled the American experience in the 1920s and 1930s. He wrote at the time, "Statistics are bloodless things." The bloodless statistics from the Great Depression are hard to fathom:

- The unemployment rate hit nearly 25%.
- GDP contracted by almost 30%.
- There were more than 9,000 bank failures.
- Corporate profits fell by 70%.
- By 1933, more than 40% of all mortgages were in default.
- Wages dropped by 60%.
- In 1929, more than 90% of U.S. companies made a profit. That fell to less than 39% by 1933.
- Economic production didn't hit 1929 levels again until 1941 thanks to the Second World War.

The 1930s were filled with breadlines. People couldn't find jobs. Cash was scarce. Many people couldn't buy food or pay their bills. Businesses couldn't pay workers, and banks wouldn't accept checks they couldn't cash immediately. Hooverville settlements of makeshift shacks constructed of boxes and scraps were set up on the outskirts of cities on vacant lots. The marriage rate and birth rate fell. Divorces also declined during the Great Depression because couples couldn't afford to split up.

There was a story about a doctor who smoothed out a single dollar bill on his desk. It was the only money he had taken in for an entire week of work. Teachers went without pay because the banks had no money in their vaults. In the spring of 1932, a crowd of some 50 men were fighting over a garbage can of leftovers in the back of a restaurant. People were literally fighting for scraps of food.

The never-ending depression

The most painful aspect of the 1930s was the sheer length of the economic pain that was seemingly never-ending. The recession itself lasted three years and seven months, but the shockwaves were felt for years after the Great Depression. Out of a U.S. population of roughly 123 million, 13 million people were out of work by 1933. The average number of unemployed workers only fell below 8 million once in the entirety of the 1930s, and that was briefly in 1937 before the onset of yet another recession and stock market crash. By 1938, the unemployment rate was still 20%.

Benjamin Roth was a young lawyer in Ohio during the Great Depression and he kept a journal of his experiences throughout the 1930s. In the summer of 1931, Roth wrote, "It hardly seems possible that things could get worse." In the spring of 1933, he went back to that original prediction, noting, "This was a poor guess. Conditions in 1932 were much worse."

The stock market had gained nearly 190% from 1933 to 1936, but the recovery wouldn't last. The stock market was cut in half, falling more than 50% during the 1937 crash. From 1929 to 1941, the U.S. stock market finished down in nine out of 13 years. That 13-year period saw stocks down 35% in total, an annual return of -3.3% for nearly a decade and a half.

The Great Depression didn't truly end until the Second World War started and the war-time spending boom kicked in. The Roaring Twenties were a killer party no one wanted to leave. The 1930s were the hangover that wouldn't quit. The crash was one of biblical proportions that would create an entire generation of investors who didn't trust the stock market.

So that settles it. This level of risk to the stock market and the economy makes investing in stocks far too dangerous over the long run, right?

Not so fast, my friend.

Buy and hold gives you the good with the bad, the ups with the downs and the booms with the busts. The U.S. stock market was up 10% per year from 1928 to 2024. Those returns include the Great Depression. They include the 86% crash. They include the lost decade of the 1930s. Those long-term returns are warts and all.

Let's say we take out some of those bad times. From 1932 to 2024, the stock market earned annual returns of 11.1% per year. If you start after the Second World War in 1950, it jumps to 11.5% annually. That's better, but it's incredible how the U.S. stock market could experience such wonderful results even when you include the worst economic and stock market event in its history. It's also incredible that you only get around a one percentage point difference in long-term annual returns by taking out the Great Depression crash.

Stocks for the long run depend on your time horizon. There will always be volatility over the short term. You could even experience godawful returns over a decade. But when you have a multi-decade time horizon, the compounding you experience in the stock market can be incredible.

In the next chapter, we'll put the Great Depression into perspective for long-term investors.

8.
NORMAL ACCIDENTS IN THE STOCK MARKET

"Another lesson I learned early is that there is nothing new in Wall Street. There can't be because speculation is as old as the hills. Whatever happens in the stock market today has happened before and will happen again."

—JESSE LIVERMORE

W HEN PRESIDENT JOHN F. KENNEDY declared in 1961 that the United States would put a man on the moon, it was a pipe dream. The government had no rockets, launchpads, spacesuits, computers or knowledge about what it would take to land on the moon. And it wasn't simply a lack of resources – experts had never studied the problem before so no one even knew what they didn't know. Scientists didn't have a clue what the course would be even if they had all of those resources.

NASA spent just $1 million on the space program in 1961 when Kennedy made his bold proclamation. Five years later they were spending $1 million every three hours on the Apollo missions. There were 14 manned Apollo missions in total, the most famous being Apollo 11 when Neil Armstrong and company took one giant leap for mankind by first stepping foot on the moon.

Apollo 13 was more infamous because it never completed its journey. Halfway to the moon, an oxygen tank exploded, stranding astronauts Jim Lovell, Jack Swigert, and Fred Haise in space and knocking out the spacecraft's primary source of oxygen. The blast was so powerful it was visible from Earth. This was the first disaster of its kind, and the crew had no idea what had happened. They had trained for countless scenarios, but nothing this catastrophic. Swigert later remarked, "Nobody thought the spacecraft would lose two fuel cells and two oxygen tanks. It couldn't happen. If somebody had thrown that at us in the simulator, we'd have said, 'Come on, you're not being realistic.'"

A spacecraft is an intricate web of interdependent components and variables. One malfunction can trigger a cascade of additional problems. Within an hour of the explosion, it became clear the moon landing was out of the question. Getting the astronauts home was now the only priority.

NASA thrives on checklists, but the checklist they now needed didn't exist. Hundreds of experts on the ground had to invent solutions on the fly, working around the clock. They tried to stay calm under pressure, though one NASA employee later admitted that "a lot of stomachs were turning over."

The astronauts moved into the Lunar Module which was originally designed for the moon landing. It became a makeshift lifeboat after the main spacecraft lost power and life support. Using the Moon's gravity as a slingshot, they figured out a course to make it home. Despite near-freezing temperatures and limited power, water, and oxygen, the astronauts executed the new plan to perfection. The crew splashed down safely in the Pacific Ocean and were rescued by the USS Iwo Jima.

Normal accidents and complex systems

Sociologist Charles Perrow calls what happened on the Apollo 13 spacecraft a "normal accident." Perrow spent his career studying accidents that occurred at nuclear power plants, airplanes and large ships at sea. Perrow argues that in highly complex and interconnected systems, failures are bound to happen due to the unpredictable interactions between the different components at play. These accidents are "normal" in the sense that they are an inherent part of the system's design, rather than being caused solely by human error or technical failure. And the more complex these systems become, the more prone they are to accidents. Perrow explains:

> As systems grow in size and in the number of diverse functions they serve, and are built to function in ever more hostile environments, increasing their ties to other systems, they experience more and more vulnerable to unavoidable system accidents.
>
> We construct an expected world because we can't handle the complexity of the present one, and then process the information that fits the expected world, and find reasons to exclude the information that might contradict it. Unexpected or unlikely interactions are ignored when we make our construction.

The Apollo 13 spacecraft was a marvel of engineering, but its complexity made it inherently prone to an accident no one could have possibly foreseen. There are few actions more complex than sending astronauts to the moon. It requires precise calculations, state-of-the-art technology and an unmatched level of planning, training and detail.

Perrow says normal accidents will occur within complex systems like this, even if you try to make them safer.

Just as the Apollo 13 disaster demonstrated the unpredictable nature of complex systems, the same forces of interdependence, rapid changes, and unforeseeable events make accidents in the stock market inevitable too. You should expect normal accidents in the financial markets on occasion.

Trying to eliminate risk when dealing with the markets is a futile exercise because risk never completely goes away; it just changes shape. Perrow cautioned against the idea of trying to eliminate risk when he wrote, "Risk can never be eliminated from high-risk systems, and we will never eliminate more than a few systems at best. At the very least, however, we stop blaming the wrong people and the wrong factors, and stop trying to fix the systems in ways that only make them riskier."

The greatest normal accident in the history of the markets was the Great Depression. And like most complex systems that fail, there was plenty of blame to go around.

What caused the Great Depression?

Finance is a complex, interconnected system and it's never just one variable that causes the collapse. The Federal Reserve bungled its role as lender of last resort by implementing overly restrictive monetary policy during a rapidly slowing economy. The Hoover administration made many policy mistakes as well. Governments around the globe placed tariffs on commodities and devalued their currencies following the First World War. The gold standard was too rigid. There were too few rules and regulations in place for the banking sector. Households had no financial backstop from the government and no protection from financial predators. There was no unemployment insurance or Social Security checks to rely on. Consumers also borrowed too much money.

My favorite explanation of the Great Depression comes from

financial humorist Fred Schwed in his classic book *Where Are the Customers' Yachts?*:

> In 1929, there was a luxurious club car which ran each week-day morning into Pennsylvania Station. Near the door there was placed a silver bowl with a quantity of nickels in it. Those who needed a nickel* in change for the subway ride downtown took one. They were not expected to put anything back in exchange; this was not money – it was one of those minor conveniences like a quill toothpick for which nothing is charged. It was only five cents.
>
> There have been many explanations of the sudden debacle of October, 1929. The explanation I prefer is that the eye of Jehovah, a wrathful god, happened to chance in October upon that bowl. In sudden understandable annoyance, Jehovah kicked over the financial structure of the United States, and thus saw to it that the bowl of free nickels disappeared forever.

The fear of the First World War and the Spanish Flu pandemic led to the euphoria of the Roaring Twenties. And the euphoria of the 1920s led to the Great Depression and its aftermath. Crashes in the stock market are inevitable because human nature is inevitable. Normal accidents are bound to occur in the stock market because human nature – fear, greed, panic and euphoria – is the one constant across all market cycles.

There are so many competing opinions, goals, time horizons and investment styles that the stock market is bound to be knocked off its axis from time to time. Financial panics and stock market crashes are a feature, not a bug, and they're never going away. However, just because crashes are inevitable does not mean you should forgo investing in the stock market.

---

* A nickel in 1929, adjusted for inflation, is worth around 90 cents today.

The best and worst 30-year returns ever

The stock market crash of 1929 to 1932 was downright nasty, but it doesn't necessarily refute the merits of long-term investing. Yes, the stock market was bludgeoned to the tune of an 80%+ wipeout. Yes, stock market investors earned a negative return for the entire decade of the 1930s. Yes, it took many years for investors to break even.

But for investors who measured their time horizon in decades rather than years, they would have made it out just fine. Honestly!

Figure 8.1 shows the annual 30-year rolling returns for the U.S. stock market going back to 1926.

Figure 8.1: S&P 500 30-year returns (1926–2024)

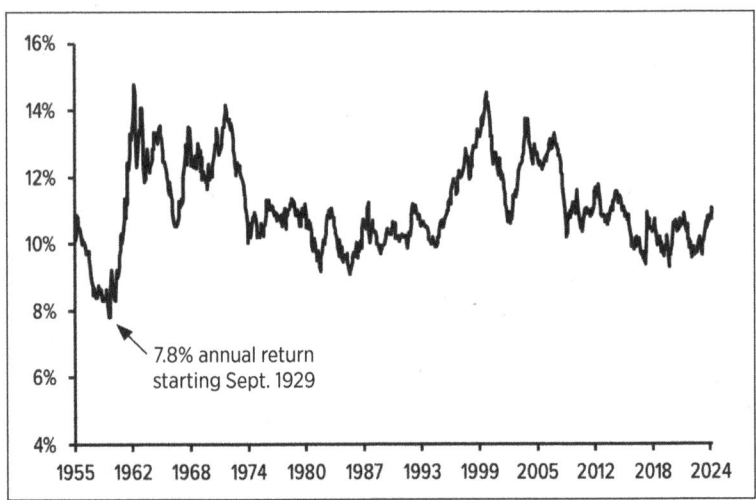

Source: Dimensional Fund Advisors (Returns 2.0).

The worst 30-year return in that time was a cumulative gain (including dividends reinvested) of a little more than 850%. That's good enough for an annual return of 7.8% per year.*

---

* This return does not include things like fees, trading costs, taxes or inflation. It's also true that reinvesting dividends was much harder back then.

To repeat, the *worst* 30-year return over the past 100 years or so of U.S. stock market data was a total gain of more than 850%. Time is your friend in the stock market.

That 30-year period ending in the summer of 1959 just so happened to start in September 1929. The onset of the Great Depression was the worst starting point in stock market history (so far), yet those returns would have turned $10,000 invested into nearly $100,000 when all was said and done. The hard part is you would have seen that initial $10,000 fall to less than $2,000 to get there.

Interestingly enough, the highest 30-year return of all time came less than three years later, at the depths of the crash in 1932, with annual returns of 15% per year for three decades. The worst entry point in stock market history quickly turned into the best entry point in a few short years.

And while it is true the stock market didn't breach the 1929 all-time highs again until 1954, the breakeven, when you include dividends reinvested, came much sooner for real-life investors.

Breaking even

The math of breaking even in the stock market is not pretty at times. If you lose 50% of your money, it requires a return of 100% just to be made whole. If you lose 86% of your investment, the return required to break even is more than 600%. From the summer of 1932 through the summer of 1945, the U.S. stock market was up around 600% in total, recouping all of the losses from the Great Crash. That was good enough for annual returns of more than 16% per year. A lost decade-plus is no fun, but that's a remarkable comeback considering the size of the crash.

I don't know if the U.S. stock market will ever experience a calamity of Great Depression-like proportions again. The government has learned from the mistakes of the past and is better equipped to handle financial crises when they hit. The U.S. economy is far more mature, dynamic and diversified; markets are more professionalized; and the

Fed has more power to step in as the lender of last resort than it did in the 1930s. But even if we don't experience a cataclysmic 80% crash in the future, there will still be corrections, bear markets and ferocious losses. Normal accidents are bound to happen when you combine the speed of information with the size and complexity of the global financial markets. The reason for the setbacks doesn't matter nearly as much as how you react to them.

Building wealth mostly happens by making good decisions ahead of time and staying out of your own way. This is why it's so important to remain dedicated to a long-term mindset during a downturn. Bear markets tempt you into thinking the days are more important than the years and the years are more important than the decades. My general investment philosophy is that the more bearish things feel in the short run, the more bullish you should be in the long run. There is no guarantee that buying stocks when they are down will lead to better outcomes, but expected returns should be higher when prices are lower.

Stock market history is littered with cycles of huge gains followed by cycles of bone-crushing losses. It has to be this way or the wonderful long-run returns wouldn't exist. If the stock market were easy everyone would be a buy-and-hold investor. The fact that it's not always easy is one of the biggest reasons the stock market goes up over the long term. It's also why true buy and hold investors succeed.

There's a scene in *Forrest Gump* where Forrest and Lieutenant Dan take their shrimp boat, *Jenny*, out to sea during a hurricane. Forrest was scared. Lieutenant Dan was angry. The storm was intense but, miraculously, their boat survived the massive storm while all the other boats were destroyed. Forrest says, "After that, shrimping was easy." That's buy and hold investing. Sometimes you have to ride out a nasty storm to find profits on the other side of it.

When you have a multi-decade time horizon the compounding you experience in the stock market can be incredible.

Now let's take a look at a short history of all the other bear markets and recessions.

9.

THE TWO TYPES OF BEAR MARKETS

*"If you spend 13 minutes a year
trying to predict the economy, you
have wasted 10 minutes."*

—PETER LYNCH

W ALL STREET PEOPLE love jargon. It gives them an air of superiority and intelligence. If you look and sound the part in the world of finance, people tend to trust you. Words like robust, granular, idiosyncratic, constructive and proprietary create a sense of importance. Finance people also love using animals when it comes to their words and phrases.

Bulls make money. Bears make money. Pigs get slaughtered.

That investment is a dog.

Dead cat bounce (more on that shortly).

Hawks, doves, butterfly spreads, iron condors, black swan events, turtle traders and more.

There are various theories about where the terms *bull market* and *bear market* came from. Some say an uptrend is called a bull market because bulls bring their horns up when they gore you. A downtrend is called a bear market because bears swipe down with their claws. There are other explanations, but this one makes sense intuitively.

Bull markets are more exciting because that's when you make money, but bear markets play the more crucial role in your long-term investment success. Surviving downturns is essential to ensure you're around to benefit from the next uptrend. There is no sunshine without nightfall, after all.

I want to look at two main types of bear markets in this chapter:

1. **Recessionary bear markets**. Market downturns that occur because of an economic slowdown.
2. **Non-recessionary bear markets**. Market downturns that occur for some other reason beyond a recession.

The difference between the two is essentially the mama bear (recessionary) versus the baby bear (non-recessionary). The mama bears tend to be bigger and badder, while the baby bears can cause some damage, sure, but the scars are typically not as deep or long-lasting.

First up, Table 9.1 shows a list of recessionary bear markets going all the way back to the Great Depression, where a bear market is defined as a peak-to-trough drawdown of 20% or worse.[*]

---

[*] For the purposes of this exercise, a bear market is over once a 20% gain takes place. And I rounded up for the 1990 bear market. Close enough.

Table 9.1: Recessionary bear markets (1928–2024)

Peak	Trough	% Decline	# of Days
9/7/29	6/1/32	−86.2%	783
9/7/32	2/27/33	−40.6%	173
7/18/33	10/21/33	−29.8%	95
3/6/37	3/31/38	−54.5%	390
6/15/48	6/13/49	−20.6%	363
7/15/57	10/22/57	−20.7%	99
12/12/61	6/26/62	−28.0%	196
11/29/68	5/26/70	−36.1%	543
1/11/73	10/3/74	−48.2%	630
11/28/80	8/12/82	−27.1%	622
7/16/90	10/11/90	−19.9%	87
3/24/00	10/9/02	−49.1%	929
10/9/07	3/9/09	−56.8%	517
2/19/20	3/23/20	−33.9%	33
Averages		−39.4%	390

Source: Bloomberg (S&P 500).

Not all of these drawdowns were the end of the world, but this list contains a who's-who of the worst crashes in history – Great Depression, 1937 crash, 1973 to 1974 bear market, bursting of the dot-com bubble, Great Financial Crisis and Covid crash.

This makes sense when you consider people lose their jobs during a recession. Companies go out of business. People lose money and stop spending as much. Profits slow and businesses contract. It doesn't take a genius to figure out why the stock market tends to fall precipitously during a collapse in economic activity.*

---

* It is worth mentioning that not every recession leads to an earth-shattering crash. The recessionary bear markets in 1990, 1980 to 1982, 1961 to 1962, 1957, and 1948 to 1949. all saw losses of less than 30%. It is possible to have a recession that leads to a relatively minor bear market.

The average recessionary bear market resulted in a loss of almost 40% and lasted well over a year (as shown in the bottom row of Table 9.1). Imagine you have a $1 million stock portfolio that falls to $600,000. Seeing your money essentially evaporate like that is painful.

Next, let's look at the non-recessionary bear markets.

Table 9.2 shows that plenty of bear markets have occurred outside of a recession. There have been 11 non-recessionary bear markets since 1928.*

Table 9.2: Non-recessionary bear markets (1928–2024)

Peak	Trough	% Decline	# of Days
2/6/34	3/14/35	−31.8%	401
10/25/39	6/10/40	−31.9%	229
11/9/40	4/28/42	−34.5%	535
5/29/46	10/9/46	−26.6%	133
2/9/66	10/7/66	−22.2%	240
8/25/87	12/4/87	−33.5%	101
7/16/90	10/11/90	−19.9%	87
7/17/98	8/31/98	−19.3%	45
4/29/11	10/3/11	−19.4%	157
9/20/18	12/24/18	−19.8%	95
1/3/22	10/12/22	−25.4%	282
Averages		**−25.8%**	**210**

Source: Bloomberg (S&P 500).

The average peak-to-trough drawdown was around 26%, lasting for roughly seven months (210 days) before bottoming.

Comparing the data on the two types of bear markets, you can see that bear markets outside of a recession tend to be shallower and

---

* Again, I rounded up to include the four bear markets where the peak-to-trough decline was 19% or more.

less lengthy, while recessionary bears are greater in magnitude and duration. Table 9.3 provides the tale of the tape comparing the two types of bear markets going back to the late 1920s.

Table 9.3: The two types of bear markets (1928–2024)

	Recessionary	Non-Recessionary
No. of Bear Markets	14	11
Average Drawdown	−39.4%	−25.8%
Average Length	390 Days	210 Days

Source: Bloomberg (S&P 500).

There have been 25 bear markets over the past 100 years, meaning they happen once every four years or so, on average. The hard part is you can't set your watch to this schedule, because there are times when bear markets cluster close together and other times when they don't happen nearly as often. For example, following the 1973 to 1974 massacre, there wasn't another bear market until 1982. After the shallow bear market in 1990, there wasn't another big decline until 1998. On the other hand, the 1930s were littered with bear markets and crashes. There were six bears in total in that decade. There were also four separate bear markets in the 1940s.

These crashes look easy to navigate with the benefit of hindsight because you know when they ended. But living through them is another story. It always feels like it's too soon to buy but too late to sell because of the dreaded dead cat bounce.

The dead cat bounce

There's an old saying that the stock market takes the stairs up but the elevator down. And while it's true that stocks tend to fall much faster than they rise, the pattern of volatility during a downturn can play head games with you. Jerry Seinfeld once joked, "Breaking up is like pushing over a Coke machine. You can't do it in one push. You gotta rock it back and forth a few times and then it goes over."

That's a good analogy for many stock market crashes too. History's great crashes are full of head-fake rallies that offered investors a false sense of hope that proved to be fleeting.

During the stock market crash that triggered the Great Depression, there was an impressive 47% rally from late 1929 to early spring 1930, following the initial plunge. Prior to that rally, stocks had already dropped 45%. The 1929–32 crash was marked by extreme volatility, including monthly gains of 8%, 9%, 12%, and 14%, as well as brief rallies of 23%, 27%, and 35% at various stages. With each rebound, investors hoped the worst was over, only to face yet another downward spiral. The stock market can be a cruel mistress indeed.

The bear market from 2000 to 2002 experienced four separate rallies of around 20% before ultimately bottoming out more than 50% below its peak. Even after hitting the lowest point, and seeing a quick 20% recovery, the market endured another 15% decline before finally beginning a sustained upward trend.

On a spreadsheet, market crashes may appear as though they move in a straight line downward, but in reality, they are usually far more erratic. Figure 9.1 shows the various rallies that occurred during the 2000 to 2002 crash.

Figure 9.1: Dead cat bounces in the 2000 to 2002 crash

Source: Bloomberg (S&P 500).

There's a good reason why it's so difficult to tell the difference between a dead cat bounce within the context of a bear market from an actual bottom. When stocks eventually bottom, they do tend to see strong gains coming out of the gate. Coming out of a bear market it's off to the races, which feels exactly the same as a dead cat bounce when you're living through it!

Table 9.4 shows the returns three and six months out from S&P 500 bear market bottoms since 1950.

Table 9.4: Returns from the bottom of bear markets since 1950

Bottom	Losses	+3 Months	+6 Months
10/22/57	−20.7%	6.7%	9.8%
6/26/62	−28.0%	6.6%	20.5%
10/7/66	−22.2%	14.6%	21.4%
5/26/70	−36.1%	17.2%	20.8%
10/3/74	−48.2%	14.0%	29.9%
3/6/78	−19.4%	15.2%	19.3%
8/12/82	−27.1%	36.2%	41.6%
12/4/87	−33.5%	20.2%	19.3%
10/11/90	−19.9%	6.2%	28.7%
8/31/98	−19.3%	22.4%	28.2%
10/9/02	−49.1%	19.2%	12.2%
3/9/09	−56.8%	38.8%	50.2%
10/3/11	−19.4%	16.5%	28.6%
12/24/18	−19.8%	20.6%	23.9%
3/23/20	−33.9%	36.3%	45.1%
10/12/22	−25.4%	11.8%	15.9%
Averages	**−29.9%**	**18.9%**	**26.0%**

Source: YCharts (S&P 500).

In 13 out of the 16 bear markets there was a double-digit return in the first three months from the bottom. All but one time saw double-digit growth six months out, while 11 times stocks were up 20% or more. I'm sure every one of these recoveries was called a dead cat bounce or bear market rally in the moment. Fool me once shame on you. Fool me twice shame on me.

Long bear markets can be psychologically challenging because they give you a glimmer of hope and then squash it. The stock market can move hard and fast in both a dead cat bounce and a bear market bottom. The true nature of these bounces will only be known in hindsight, which is one of the reasons timing the market is nearly impossible.

Volatility clusters

Stock market cycles are often driven by some combination of regret and herding. Research shows investors hold onto losing stocks too long in hopes they will come back to their original price while selling their winners too early. Investors also anchor to recent results, so initially markets underreact to news, events or data releases.

On the flip side, once things become more apparent, investors herd and overreact, causing an overshoot in either direction. Fear, greed, overconfidence and confirmation bias can lead investors to pile into winning areas of the market after they've risen or pile out after they've fallen.

These feelings get taken to another level when the market is going down and you're losing money. Table 9.5 presents a list of the top 15 best and worst days for the U.S. stock market since 1928.

Table 9.5: The best and worst days since 1928

Losses	Date	Gains	Date
−20.5%	October 19, 1987	16.6%	March 15, 1933
−13.0%	October 28, 1929	12.5%	October 30, 1929
−12.0%	March 16, 2020	12.4%	October 6, 1931
−10.2%	October 29, 1929	11.9%	September 5, 1939
−9.9%	November 6, 1929	11.8%	September 21, 1932
−9.5%	March 12, 2020	11.6%	October 13, 2008
−9.1%	October 18, 1937	10.8%	October 28, 2008
−9.1%	October 5, 1931	10.5%	June 22, 1931
−9.0%	October 5, 2008	9.5%	April 20, 1933
−8.9%	December 1, 2008	9.4%	March 24, 2020
−8.9%	July 20, 1933	9.3%	March 13, 2020
−8.8%	September 29, 2008	9.3%	August 8, 1932
−8.7%	July 21, 1933	9.1%	October 21, 1987
−8.6%	October 10, 1932	9.0%	November 14, 1929
−8.3%	October 26, 1987	8.9%	June 19, 1933

Source: YCharts (S&P 500).

It's no accident that some of the worst days in stock market history happened during major crashes. More than half of the worst days took place in and around the Great Depression, while three of the 15 biggest down days came in 2008. What is surprising is the fact that the best days in history also took place amid those very same downturns. Two-thirds of the best days occurred during the 1930s while two of the biggest up days were in the fall of 2008 as the financial system was crumbling. This is not a coincidence.

Bull markets tend to be relatively boring. It's not giant leaps forward but more of a slow, methodical move higher. This is why there aren't many headlines about bull markets unless the Dow crosses a nice round number. Progress takes time so the distribution of daily returns is relatively tight. Investors get lulled into a false sense of confidence.

Then bear markets come along, slap you in the face, pick you up off the ground, and then kick you in the shins for good measure. The biggest down days *and* up days typically occur during downtrends when investor emotions are heightened. In downward-trending markets, price movements are highly unpredictable, with wild swings in both directions. Panic selling and panic buying drive short-term volatility spikes both ways. The fear, anxiety, and panic that accompany these periods lead to overreactions, as the pain of losing money is so overwhelming.

Mr. Market

In his classic book *The Intelligent Investor*, Benjamin Graham describes short-term market fluctuations through a parable about an obliging business partner named Mr. Market. Each day, Mr. Market shows up to tell you what he thinks your investment is worth and offers to either buy your shares or sell you his stake in the company. Some days, Mr. Market is overly enthusiastic and offers you far more money than your shares are worth. Other days, Mr. Market is depressed and offers you substantially less than your shares are worth. Regardless, he shows up every day when the market is open to offer you a new price.

The good news is that you can choose when to engage with Mr. Market to buy or sell. If his offers aren't appealing, you're not obligated to accept them. Wise investors understand you should ignore Mr. Market on most occasions. In the short run, the stock market is a walking contradiction – cruel, heartless, and wildly unpredictable. Basing investment decisions on Mr. Market's erratic mood swings is rarely a wise decision.

In his book *Simple Wealth, Inevitable Wealth*, Nick Murray compares the stock market to the planting of a tree. It takes time for trees to grow and take root. Trees require oxygen, water, sunlight and patience to reach their full potential. But you don't dig up the tree to check its progress every few months. Murray explains, "Give the tree enough room, enough light, and enough time. Then leave it pretty much alone." Successful investing requires a good deal of patience, discipline and letting your investments grow too.

In *The Four Pillars of Investing*, William Bernstein shares a metaphor from portfolio manager Ralph Wanger that brilliantly illustrates the stock market's behavior. Wanger compares the stock market to a man walking his dog. While the man moves steadily toward his destination, the dog darts back and forth unpredictably on its leash. The dog's movements are erratic and rapid, but the man maintains a slow, steady pace, always progressing in the right direction. In this analogy, the man represents the stock market in the long run, while the dog symbolizes its short-term volatility. Everyone pays attention to the dog while the owner's path is the only one that matters.

The hard part is you don't know when Mr. Market is going to change his mood. You don't know when it's time to prune some tree branches. You don't know when the man will reach his destination or when the dog wants a breather in the shade. It takes an iron will to invest in the stock market because Mr. Market is a manic-depressive who wants you to chop down your tree too early and follow the dog instead of the man holding the leash.

Every time stocks drop a little, it feels like they could drop a lot more. When they enter a correction, it feels like a bear market could be next. And when they slip into a bear market, it feels like they will surely spiral into an all-out crash. In these market environments, you should go long humility and short hubris. The emotional pendulum of the stock market swings in both directions from fear to greed, panic to euphoria and back again. The problem is that it's impossible to predict how far it will swing in either direction in advance.

How to prepare for a bear market

How you prepare for bear markets depends greatly on where you are in your investing lifecycle.

If you're retired, nearing retirement or have a mature portfolio, you don't always have the luxury of waiting out a prolonged bear market. Diversification and liquidity can help because you don't have as much time to ride out a storm or as much income to buy more stocks at depressed prices. Cash and short-term bonds can act as a drag on long-term returns, but can ensure that you won't be out of luck when you need to spend down your portfolio.

On the other hand, a bear market is a gift for younger investors who have decades ahead of them to save and invest. If you'll be a net saver in the years ahead, stock market corrections and crashes are a buying opportunity. They allow you to buy stocks at discounted prices, lower valuations, and higher dividend yields. A long time horizon and consistent investing can help you tame even the most grizzly of bear markets. You just have to have the intestinal fortitude to keep buying stocks at the worst times.

Bear markets are a normal part of market cycles. The reasons vary, but the emotions are always the same. No one can predict how long they'll last, but they do come to an end, and life goes on. You just need a solid handle on your risk profile and time horizon in the meantime.

In the next chapter, we'll look at the uneven relationship between the stock market and the economy.

10.

THE STOCK MARKET VS. THE ECONOMY

"An economist is an expert who will know
tomorrow why the things he predicted
yesterday didn't happen today."

−LAURENCE J. PETER

THE WHOLE IDEA of "the economy" as we know it today is relatively new. In fact, the concept of gross domestic product (GDP) as a way to measure economic growth wasn't developed until the aftermath of the Great Depression.

Simon Kuznets, an economist who won the Nobel Prize for his work in this area, submitted a report to U.S. Congress in 1934 in which he used a concept called national income to track economic activity. GDP was born out of this idea, but it didn't become the standard methodology used by countries around the globe until the end of the Second World War.

Once economists were able to measure economic output, they could calculate the damage previous downturns had caused to the economy. They calculated that in the 1800s there were 18 recessions in addition to six panics or depressions. The National Bureau of Economic Research (NBER), the organization responsible for officially declaring recessions, lists the longest GDP contraction on record at 65 months, from October 1873 to March 1879, in what is known as the Long Depression.*

After a land price boom-bust in the early 1800s, the word *panic* entered the lexicon to describe speculative economic episodes that resulted in a spectacular collapse. Panic was used for the remainder of the century to describe what is now termed a depression. Government officials decided they needed something less alarming to the public, which is how the term *recession* came to be used to describe economic downturns of varying severity.

From the start of the 1930s until halfway through the 2020s, the U.S. economy spent 185 months – 16% of the time – in the throes of recession. Alternatively, this means that 84% of the time the economy was not in a recession and was thus in an expansion or treading water.

My general investing philosophy is that the stock market usually goes up, but sometimes it goes down. You can make a similar claim about the U.S. economy. Most of the time the economy is growing, but sometimes it shrinks.

For both the economy and the stock market, it is foolish to assume the good times will last forever. The good times are usually followed by bad times.

The hard part about financial markets and the economy is that it's nearly impossible to predict when and *how badly* things will end. Or if they will end at all...

---

* In comparison, the Great Depression of 1929 to 1932 was 43 months long.

Predicting recessions is hard

The 2020s experienced one of the biggest economic shocks in history. When the pandemic struck in early 2020, we essentially turned off the economy and then turned it back on again like a Nintendo. Millions of people began working from home with no advance notice. Businesses shut down. Oil prices went negative. Millions of people lost their jobs. Figure 10.1 shows how the unemployment rate spiked from 3.5% to a historically high level of 14.7% within the space of two months in early 2020.

Figure 10.1: U.S. unemployment rate (1960–2024)

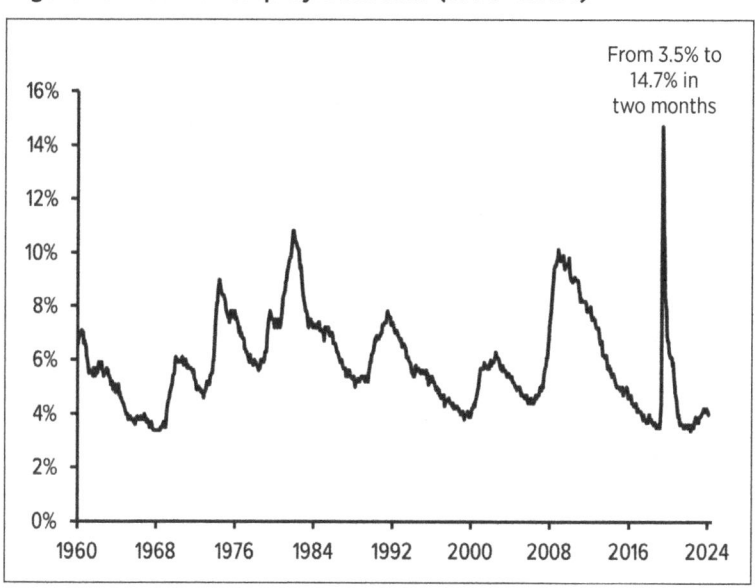

Source: YCharts.com.

The Covid-induced recession of early 2020 will go down as one of the most unusual economic contractions in history. Lasting just two months, it saw the steepest quarterly GDP decline since the Great Depression. NBER didn't acknowledge the start of the February

2020 downturn until June of that year. Frankly, we didn't need official confirmation to know a recession had hit. The moment the NBA postponed its season, Tom Hanks announced he had contracted Covid, and schools nationwide shut down, it was clear a recession was right on our doorstep.

It's not always that easy.

That period of uncertainty was followed by unprecedented levels of spending from governments around the globe, supply chain shocks, and a war in Ukraine which led to the highest level of inflation in four decades.

By 2022, a recession was not just consensus – it felt obvious. It wasn't just economic models sounding the alarm. Everyone from economists to investors and pundits alike assumed it was only a matter of time before the economy slowed considerably. Prominent figures like Amazon's Jeff Bezos, JP Morgan's Jamie Dimon, and the Bond King Jeffrey Gundlach all warned of an impending recession. In fact, Bloomberg ran a headline in October 2022 that read:

Forecast For U.S. Recession Within Year Hits 100%

The recession never materialized and the economy kept growing.

How can that be? From 100% likelihood – certainty! – to not happening at all.

There are many reasons GDP kept growing, but the key takeaway is that predicting the economy's next move is a fool's errand. Even when a recession does occur, forecasting its timing and severity can be incredibly challenging.

For starters, the definition of a recession itself is difficult to pin down. Some people claim it's two consecutive negative quarterly GDP prints. NBER has its own definition:

The NBER's traditional definition of a recession is that it is a significant decline in economic activity that is spread across the economy and that lasts more than a few months. The committee's view is that while each of the three criteria – depth, diffusion, and duration – needs to be met individually to some degree, extreme conditions revealed by one criterion may partially offset weaker indications from another.

That is a lot of jargon to say, "It's complicated," which makes sense when talking about something as big, diverse and dynamic as the U.S. economy. There are billions of moving pieces. Plus, economic data is not always current like stock prices. Economic data requires estimates, surveys, updates and adjustments. With so many moving parts in the multi-trillion-dollar U.S. economy, it can be challenging to fully grasp what's happening in real time.

For example, a brief recession began in January 1980, but NBER didn't officially confirm its start until June, just one month before it ended. By the time they declared the recession had finished in July 1980, a new economic contraction had already begun in July 1981. The recession from July 1981 to November 1982 wasn't officially recognized until July of 1983. Similarly, the recession that started in the summer of 1990 wasn't officially acknowledged until the spring of 1991. NBER didn't declare the March 2001 recession until November 2001 – the same month it ended. The Great Financial Crisis, which began in December 2007, wasn't officially designated until December 2008, the same month Bernie Madoff's Ponzi scheme was exposed.

If the literal judges of what constitutes a recession can't tell when it's happening, what chance do you and I have?

Waiting for the dust to settle

Imagine I could provide you with the exact start and end dates of economic slowdowns before they occur. Would you be able to use this knowledge to earn better returns in the stock market?

Probably not.

Stock market returns before, during and after recessions are all over the place. It's not as simple as getting out before the recession, then back in when the recession is over.

Table 10.1 provides a look at every recession since the Second World War along with S&P 500 returns in the six months leading up to the recession, during the actual recession itself and then one, three, five and 10 years from the end of the recession.

Table 10.1: Stock market returns before, during and after a recession

Recession Dates	6 Months Prior	In Recession	One Year	Three Years	Five Years	Ten Years
Nov 1948– Oct 1949	9.8%	4.1%	31.5%	88.0%	171.3%	497.0%
July 1953– May 1954	−6.5%	27.6%	35.9%	83.7%	144.8%	294.4%
Aug 1957– April 1958	9.3%	−6.5%	37.3%	66.3%	89.7%	211.3%
April 1960– Feb 1961	−1.0%	18.4%	13.6%	35.1%	68.4%	111.3%
Dec 1969– Nov 1970	−7.8%	−3.5%	11.2%	20.6%	25.2%	145.9%
Nov 1973– Mar 1975	2.9%	−17.9%	28.3%	22.0%	55.3%	252.4%
Jan 1980– July 1980	7.7%	16.1%	12.9%	55.9%	100.9%	345.6%
July 1981– Nov 1982	−1.0%	14.7%	25.4%	67.2%	103.2%	350.5%
July 1990– Mar 1991	3.1%	7.6%	11.0%	29.8%	98.2%	284.7%
Mar 2001– Nov 2001	−17.8%	−7.2%	−16.5%	8.4%	34.3%	33.2%
Dec 2007– June 2009	−2.3%	−35.5%	14.4%	57.7%	137.0%	294.2%
Averages	**−0.3%**	**1.6%**	**18.7%**	**48.6%**	**93.5%**	**256.4%**

Sources: NBER, Returns 2.0 (S&P 500).

It's often said that the stock market is forward-looking, but that doesn't mean it's all knowing. In nearly half of these recessions, the stock market was up in the six months before the downturn hit. And 55% of the time the stock market rose during the actual recession itself! The biggest takeaway from this data is how wonderful the returns are coming out of an economic contraction. The three, five, and 10-year returns following an economic reset provide ample evidence that you should not get scared out of stocks just because the economy slows. Recessions are a wonderful buying opportunity.

The stock market and the economy aren't always in sync with one another. At times, the stock market front runs the economy, while other times it's slow to react to economic data. Occasionally, stocks decline as the economy contracts, and at other times they hit bottom well before the economy does.

Recessions are painful, so it's understandable that people want to time the market when a slowdown feels imminent. The problem here is twofold:

1. Predicting the timing of a recession is hard to do.
2. Predicting how and when the stock market will react to a recession is also difficult.

You could nail the timing of the recession, but whiff on the bottom of the stock market. In the eight recessions that occurred between 1950 and 2010, six of them saw the stock market bottom before the recession was over. In those instances, the stock market bottomed four to five months before the recession ended. The stock market bottoms an average of nine months before the nadir in corporate earnings in a bear market. If you wait for the dust to settle on the economy, there's a good chance the stock market will leave you behind.

The Great Financial Crisis recession technically ended in June 2009. However, the stock market bottomed in early March 2009. By the time the economy bottomed, the stock market was already up almost 40%. The S&P 500 had already zoomed nearly 60% higher by the time the unemployment rate peaked at around 10% in October 2009 and finally began its descent.

To quote Warren Buffett: "If you knew what was going to happen in the economy, you still wouldn't necessarily know what was going to happen in the stock market."

Timing the economy is hard.

Timing the stock market is harder.

The stock market vs. the economy

The stock market is mostly made up of large corporations that make things and sell things. The economy is mostly the stuff we do with those things. Most of the time the stock market and the economy are moving in the same direction, but they can and will diverge. Sometimes investors pay a high multiple of corporate profits when buying stocks and sometimes they pay a low multiple. Sometimes high economic growth leads to high stock market returns, but this relationship is not set in stone.

Take a look at the inflation-adjusted annual returns for the U.S. stock market compared to real GDP growth by decade in Table 10.2.

Table 10.2: The stock market vs. the economy

Decade	Real Stock Returns	Real GDP Growth
1930s	2.6%	0.5%
1940s	7.2%	5.8%
1950s	14.3%	4.2%
1960s	5.3%	4.5%
1970s	0.7%	3.2%
1980s	9.1%	3.1%
1990s	14.5%	3.1%
2000s	−1.0%	1.9%
2010s	12.0%	2.2%

Sources: NYU (S&P 500), FRED.

You can see that economic growth in the 1940s was higher than it was in the 1950s, but stock market returns were much better in the 1950s than the prior decade. Real GDP growth was basically the same rate in the 1970s, 1980s and 1990s. Yet the stock market performed terribly in the 1970s and went bananas in the 1980s and 1990s. Growth was subdued in each of the first two decades of the 21st century. One of those decades experienced phenomenal stock market performance while the other was dreadful.

The stock market is far more volatile than the economy, as well. Table 10.3 shows the rankings of the worst stock market drawdowns and GDP contractions in the United States since 1950.

Table 10.3: Bad times since 1950

Stock Market Downturns	GDP Contractions
−56.8%	−19.2%
−49.1%	−5.1%
−48.2%	−3.7%
−36.1%	−3.2%
−33.9%	−2.7%
−33.5%	−2.6%
−28.0%	−2.2%
−27.1%	−1.6%
−25.4%	−1.4%
−22.2%	−0.6%
−20.7%	−0.3%

Sources: NBER, Returns 2.0.

The drawdowns in the stock market are magnitudes bigger than contractions in the economy. The worst reduction in GDP is a run-of-the-mill bear market in stocks. To be fair, the stock market is a value at a point in time while the economy is how much value is produced over a period of time. Still, it's important to remember the stock market likes to freak out far more drastically than the economy.

Why does the stock market have bigger swings than the economy?

Legendary investor Howard Marks once wrote it's, "[b]ecause of the importance and unpredictability of market participants' psyches or emotions. Investor sentiment swings a great deal, swamping the short-run influence of fundamentals. It's for this reason that relatively few market forecasts prove correct, and fewer still are 'right for the right reason.'"

In other words, the stock market is volatile because people's emotions, reactions and predictions are volatile.

In the early 1980s, Professor Robert Shiller set out to answer the question: Do stock prices move too much to be justified by subsequent changes in dividends? Shiller wanted to figure out how well the stock market tracks the present value of future cash flows in the short term. In the land of textbooks, the present value of any financial asset should equate to its discounted future cash flows. If only it were that easy.

Shiller concluded that, no, stock prices do not neatly track fundamentals. In fact, the dividend stream of the stock market is not all that volatile. Cash flows don't increase or decrease nearly as much as stock prices do. Shiller noted that between September 1929 and June 1932, the inflation-adjusted S&P index fell 81%. Real dividends fell just 11% in that time. Between January 1973 and December 1974, the real S&P index was down 54%, while real dividends declined just 6%. The difference is investor emotions which go into hyperdrive during the bad times.

I have a confession to make. The title of this chapter is somewhat misleading; the stock market and the economy are not always opposed. Sometimes the stock market *is* the economy. But other times it's not. The stock market and the economy share a complex, often unpredictable relationship. While they move together over the long run, their short-term paths are shaped by countless factors – some rational, others entirely emotional. Markets swing wildly because investor sentiment swings wildly. The economy grows steadily over time, but recessions are inevitable.

I'm not trying to tell you that recessions don't matter or that stock market volatility can be completely ignored. When these things happen it can be painful. It's just that trying to guess them in advance is a losing proposition. The lovely thing about the stock market is that it allows you to ride the coattails of corporations by taking part in their profits, growth and ingenuity as they innovate and create shareholder value.

The good news is you don't have to learn how to time the market or the economy to succeed as an investor.

In the next chapter, let's talk about something even harder than timing recessions – day trading.

11.

DAY TRADING

"If you really want something in life you
have to work for it. Now quiet! They're
about to announce the lottery numbers."

—HOMER SIMPSON

D URING THE MEME stock craze of 2021, *The Wall Street Journal*
profiled a day trader who turned $500 into more than $200,000
in less than three weeks by trading options on GameStop. That's a
life-changing amount of money. This guy hit the stock market lottery.
Lucky for him, he has a responsible group of friends when it comes to
offering financial advice:

'You really need to sell,' a friend said.

He wouldn't. Some on Wall Street Bets were predicting
GameStop would hit $1,000, even $5,000. Hold tight and don't
sell, they urged. We're in this together.

Finally, his friends staged what Mr. Guha jokingly calls a
'mini intervention.' One asked if he would invest in GameStop
at the sky-high levels if he had fresh money – if not, he should
exit the trade. The argument won him over.

Over the course of the next few weeks, GameStop shares crashed nearly 90%. This is the dream scenario – get in, hit the jackpot and get out.

If only it were that easy.

The finance industry wants you to be a day trader. They want you to speculate on short-dated options, over-trade your brokerage account, gamble on leveraged ETFs and churn your portfolio until nothing is left. There are always going to be people who win the lottery, but that doesn't mean it's a strategy you should try to pull off with your life savings. Day traders face a much higher hurdle rate than long-term investors for a simple reason – **day trading is HARD**.

I know, I know, no one likes to hear about the pitfalls of overnight riches when it sounds so fun and lucrative. Wouldn't it be cool to set up six monitors at your desk, look at lines on charts all day and make bank?! Of course, but I would be remiss if I didn't share some cautionary tales for those who feel like there's easy money to be made day trading in the markets.

A study of Brazilian futures traders revealed that 97% of those who traded for over 300 days ended up losing money. Just over 1% managed to earn more than the Brazilian minimum wage ($16 per day), while only half a percent made more than a bank teller's salary ($54 per day) – all while taking on significantly greater risk. The longer these futures traders remained in the day trading casino, the more likely they were to experience losses – the opposite of long-term buy and hold investing.

A study of individual day traders in Taiwan over a 15-year span found that even the most experienced traders tended to lose money. That's not surprising – but what is surprising is that even the traders who consistently lost money continued trading through the losses. The vast majority were unprofitable, with only 5% of traders turning a profit. Those who lost money were more likely to over-trade, with unprofitable traders making up 70% to 80% of the total trading volume. If at first you don't succeed, trade, trade again.

Currency markets might be the toughest challenge for day traders there is. The forex market is highly competitive, operates 24/7, involves loads of leverage, and is influenced by all sorts of economic variables. A study by the U.S. Securities and Exchange Commission (SEC) looked at the performance of individual currency day traders. The results were dismal. Around 70% of retail forex traders lost money each quarter, and on average, a trader's entire investment was wiped out within a year. Even the "best" quarterly performance among these traders resulted in a 24% loss. It's like they were trying to lose money.

Finally, a study found that nearly 80% of eToro day traders lost money over a 12-month period. The median loss in that time was 36%.

I could continue with more results and statistics, but it feels like that would be rubbing it in at this point. No need to beat a dead horse here.

Does this mean day trading is impossible? Not necessarily. I'm sure some successful day traders do exist. The problem is these people are essentially unicorns and you are not one of them (neither am I). The longer you stay invested in the stock market, the greater your odds of experiencing gains. With day trading, the opposite is true. Much like a casino, in day trading, the house always wins.

Cocaine brain

Investing in the financial markets is like stepping onto the same basketball court as Steph Curry and LeBron James. You're not only trading with other individuals, but also institutional investors, hedge funds, professional money managers, algorithmic trading firms run by codebreakers and PhDs, and millions of other traders and investors who have more information, computing power and market knowledge than you. In the markets, you're also competing against yourself.

In *Your Money & Your Brain*, Jason Zweig explores how your brain influences and responds to financial decisions and outcomes. His findings are both alarming and enlightening.

Brain scans reveal that the neurological response to making money on investments is nearly identical to that of a person high on cocaine or morphine. The brain perceives financial gains and drug-induced highs in a similar way, so you need a bigger hit each time for the same emotional response. After experiencing a pattern just twice, the brain expects to see a third repetition automatically since we humans are pattern-seeking creatures.

Moreover, research shows that financial losses can haunt you even in your sleep – brain scans of sleeping individuals confirm that you can literally feel financial setbacks in your nightmares. Going on a financial losing streak makes it more likely you'll develop memories of fear and anxiety. These dopamine hits and serotonin blasts are all defense mechanisms that are ill-suited for investors who just want to make some money trading stocks.

A study conducted at a horse racing track examined bettors' confidence in their chosen horse before and after placing their bets. Researchers found that people became significantly more confident in their horse's chances of winning after placing their wager than they were beforehand. This phenomenon explains why day trading can be so psychologically challenging – you develop an emotional attachment to your trades to justify your positions instead of judging them by merit.

Willpower alone doesn't do the trick

Emotions themselves aren't inherently good or bad – they're just part of being human. But they do make trading incredibly challenging. Day trading subjects you to your worst impulses all the time. The more often you engage with the stock market, the more your emotions will impact your reactions in a negative way because self-control is a finite resource.

To test the limits of human self-control, researchers studied the dining behaviors of hundreds of patrons at Chinese buffets across the country to understand what influenced their consumption patterns. They found that diners ate less when using chopsticks or smaller plates. They consumed more when using forks and larger plates. Additionally, healthier individuals tended to survey the buffet before picking out what to eat, whereas unhealthy eaters grabbed everything they could fit onto their plates. Seating location also played a role – those sitting closer to the buffet ate more, while individuals facing away from the buffet line consumed much less.

Personal finance experts are enamored with equating health and wealth. After all, everyone knows how to be healthy – eat right and exercise regularly. And everyone knows how to become wealthy – stay out of credit card debt, live below your means and invest wisely. I contend that maintaining good health is far more mentally challenging than accumulating wealth.

You make over 200 food-related decisions daily, making it incredibly easy to give in to unhealthy choices – fast food, snacks, convenience store treats, food delivery apps, and deep-fried restaurant entrees. The temptations are endless. Being healthy requires constant effort. You can't put your health on autopilot. Working out requires motivation every single time you go to the gym. You also have to exercise your willpower to eat right, which is why studies estimate that 95% of dieters eventually regain the weight they lost.

Staying healthy requires daily commitment, whereas building wealth is often about making good decisions up front, sticking with them and staying out of your own way. Since knowledge alone is not enough to change behavior, wise investors put rules in place to guide their actions and automate good behavior ahead of time. Some investors need enforced smaller portion sizes, just like the buffet diners.

Scratching the itch

Each year, Americans spend more money on the lottery than on sporting events, books, video games, movie tickets and music *combined*. Some people love the thrill of gambling, speculation and the dream of hitting it big.

Many finance experts assume people should act like robots and avoid speculation altogether. I'm not naive. People are people and some of us just love to gamble. If you're one of these people who need to scratch that itch, just do so in a responsible manner. Carve out 5–10% of your portfolio as a behavioral release valve and go nuts – day-trade, time the market, take a flier on some fads, trade options, buy and sell crypto, go long biotech stocks, trade penny stocks, etc. Have as much fun as you like.

I know this is blasphemous to certain investment thinkers, but this can be a worthwhile endeavor if your 5–10% "fun" portfolio allows you to stick to a longer-term, set-it-and-forget-it investment plan with the other 90–95% of your capital. Even people on a diet need the occasional cheat day. You just have to size it right so you don't overdo it.

I had one of these side portfolios in a brokerage account where I tried my hand at stock-picking, market-timing and out-guessing the markets. It was fun for a while, but then I looked at my results and realized my fun portfolio wasn't so much fun anymore. Ten percent of my portfolio was causing 90% of my worries because I was constantly checking the performance of my account. It wasn't worth the brain drain, so I automated that account too.

Sometimes you need to face your chair away from the buffet so you're not so focused on the day-to-day in the markets or the returns of other investors with different goals and time horizons than you.

Vanguard's Jack Bogle once said, "This is one of the most important rules of investing. If you never peek from the age of 20 to the age of 70, you'll rip that first 401(k) statement open at age 70, and I recommend you have a doctor on hand because you'll go into a dead faint. Your heart might even stop. You're going to have an amount of money you can't even imagine."

That's not entirely realistic, but he's directionally right. As long as you're saving and investing on a periodic basis, paying more attention to your portfolio is not going to make it grow any faster. In fact, the opposite is true. The more you handle a bar of soap the smaller it gets.

The same is true with your investments. The odds are stacked against you as a day trader and you're probably not going to get rich overnight.

In the next chapter, let's take a look at why volatility is your friend, not a risk like so many investors are often inclined to believe.

12.

VOLATILITY IS A FEATURE, NOT A BUG

"In the world of finance, the only black swans
are the history that investors have not read."

—WILLIAM BERNSTEIN

ROGER FEDERER IS in the conversation for the greatest tennis player of all time. He won over 100 professional titles, including 20 major championships, which amounted to more than $130 million in prize money. Federer was the world's top-ranked male tennis player for 310 weeks during his illustrious career.

U.S. tennis star Andy Roddick once admitted, "My life on the line, he's [Federer] the last guy I'd want to play."

However, Federer's opponents won plenty of points against him. They even won some sets. But it was rare they beat him in an entire match. In a commencement speech to Dartmouth graduates shortly after he retired, Federer reflected on his career with some mind-blowing numbers that bear this out:

In tennis, perfection is impossible. In the 1,526 singles matches I played in my career, I won almost 80% of those matches. Now, I have a question for all of you: What percentage of the POINTS do you think I won in those matches?

Only 54%.

In other words, even top-ranked tennis players win barely more than half of the points they play.

When you lose every second point, on average, you learn not to dwell on every shot.

You teach yourself to think: OK, I double-faulted. It's only a point.

OK, I came to the net and I got passed again. It's only a point.

Federer won 80% of his matches, but only 54% of the points in those matches.

One of the most dominant tennis players ever won most of his matches, but not always in dominating fashion. It was more like slight advantages over the short run that compounded through consistency over the long run.

When I heard this speech, my finance brain immediately went to the stock market. Federer's win rates are basically the same as that of the stock market!

On a daily basis going back to the 1920s, the S&P 500 has been positive roughly 52% of the time, very close to Federer's individual point win rate of 54%. The daily win rate of the stock market isn't much better than a flip of the coin, as shown in Figure 12.1.

Figure 12.1: Daily win rate for the U.S. stock market (S&P 500, 1928–2024)

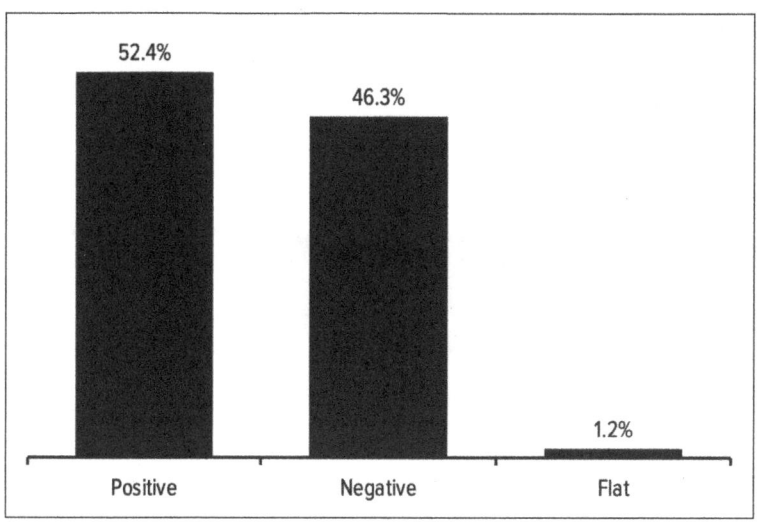

Source: Bloomberg.

Small edges add up in the stock market too. The average daily gain in the U.S. stock market going back to 1928 is just 0.03%. This is shown in Figure 12.2.

Figure 12.2: Average daily gains and losses for the U.S. stock market (S&P 500, 1928–2024)

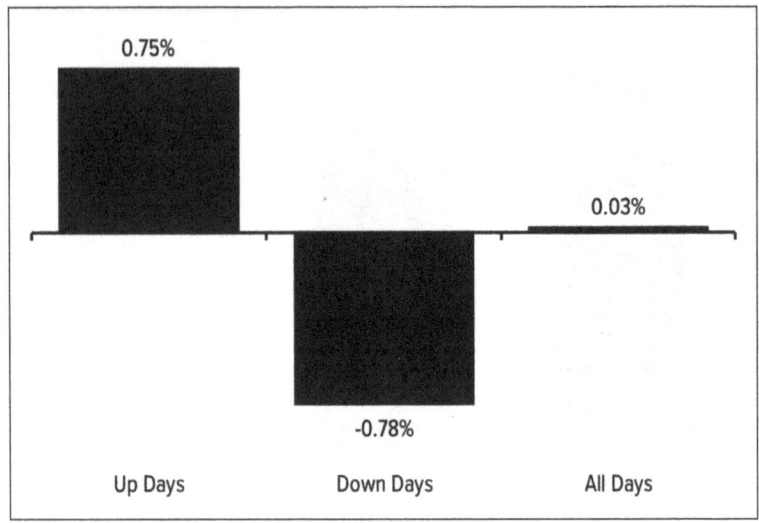

Source: Bloomberg.

These figures reflect price-only returns, excluding dividends. On a price-only basis, the S&P 500 was up close to 39,000% from 1928 to 2024. From 0.03% each day to 39,000% over 96 years. And when you factor in reinvested dividends, the total return skyrockets to an astonishing 982,000%. No one actually has an investing time horizon that long, but the benefits of compounding small daily gains in the stock market can be truly remarkable.

If Roger Federer gave up every time he lost a point, he wouldn't have 20 grand slam titles. Likewise, if you put too much weight on short-term outcomes in the stock market, you're not going to succeed as an investor. You must be willing to lose some points in the short term to win some matches in the long term. Volatility is the price of admission.

The best casino ever

Investors often compare the stock market to a casino, but that analogy never made sense to me. In an actual casino the house has the edge, so the longer you play, the higher your probability of losing. The stock market is the opposite.

Some people blindly assume the stock market is rigged. Yes, the stock market is rigged against you if you're looking for easy money. But it's also rigged in favor of long-term investors. This is because the win rate in the stock market increases the longer you play.

Looking at post-Second World War data starting in 1950, the win rates for the S&P 500 over the long run are phenomenal (see Figure 12.3)!

Figure 12.3: Stock market win rate by holding period (S&P 500, 1950-2024)

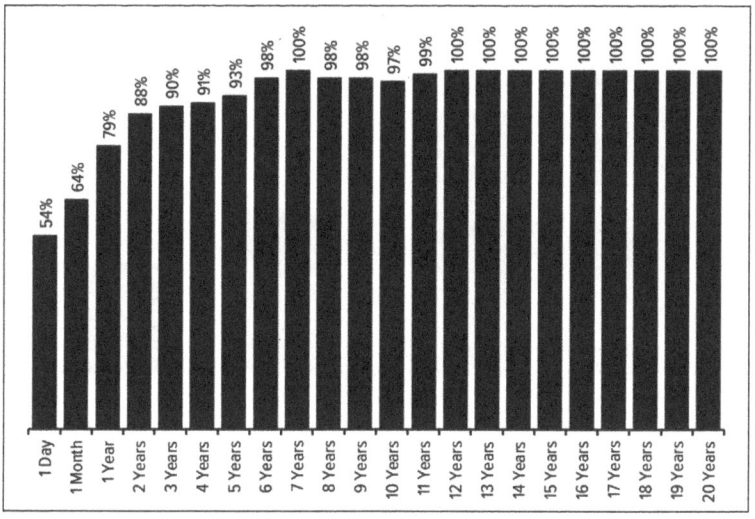

Source: Returns 2.0.

The win rates increase from a little better than a coin flip on a one-day time horizon to quickly above 90% for holding periods of more than three years. It's remarkable to consider the U.S. stock market was never down over any 12-year window in this 75 years of data. And although there were some lost decades (more on this in Chapter 17), the stock market was positive in 97% of all 10-year total returns.

Minor advantages that compound over long time horizons can do wonders for your wealth. Despite this fact, you have to survive volatility to earn these wonderful results. To repeat my stock market philosophy: Most of the time the stock market goes up but sometimes it goes down. Losses are a feature, not a bug.

For example, you're highly likely to experience a correction in a given year in the stock market, as shown in Figure 12.4.

Figure 12.4: Percentage of years with stock market losses (S&P 500, 1928–2024)

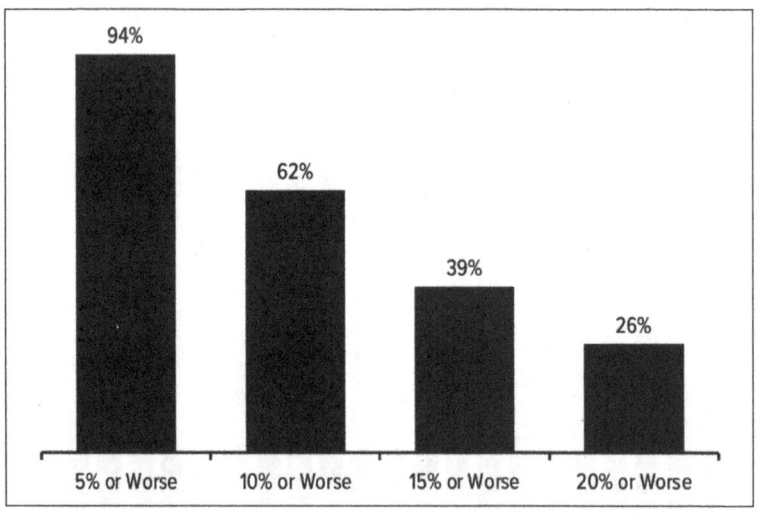

Source: Returns 2.0.

This chart shows that nearly two-thirds of the time, there has been a double-digit correction at some point in a given calendar year. Just 6% of all years since 1928 have seen a maximum peak-to-trough drawdown of less than 5%.

Interestingly, even when the stock market has experienced a correction, it's likely the market still finishes the year with gains. Figure 12.5 shows the calendar year returns along with the peak-to-trough drawdowns for the S&P 500.

Figure 12.5: Stock market calendar year returns and peak-to-trough drawdowns (S&P 500, 1928–2024)

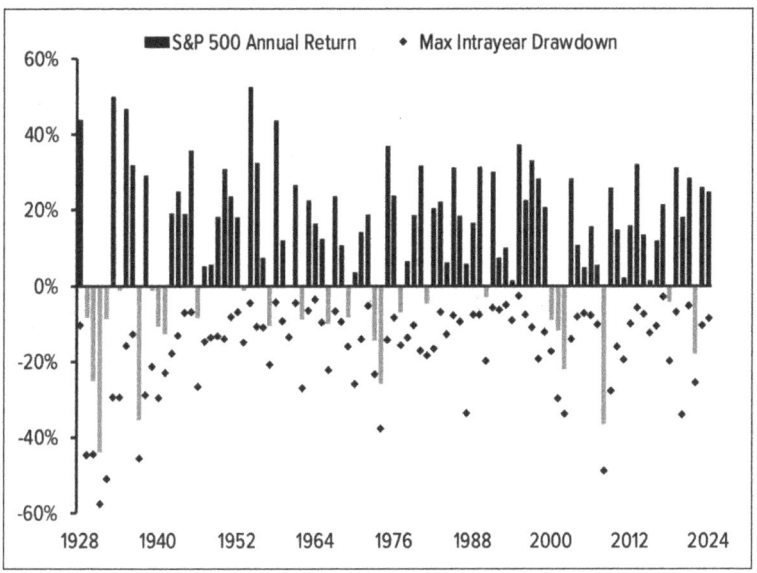

Source: YCharts.com.

The average peak-to-trough drawdown during a given calendar year from 1928 to 2024 was -16.3%. In 35 of the 61 years with a double-digit correction, the S&P 500 still finished the year in positive territory.

Allow me to repeat that – out of the 61 years with a correction of 10% or worse, the stock market still finished the year with gains in 57% of those years. And 24 of those 31 up years had a year-end gain of 10% or more! That means two out of every five years with a double-digit correction at some point along the way still finished with double-digit gains.

In that same time frame, the stock market experienced 36 years with gains of 20% or more. Out of those 36 years, there has been a correction of 10% or worse on the way to those gains in 17 years. So in almost half of all years when the U.S. stock market was up 20% or more, there has been a double-digit correction during the journey to those wonderful gains.

Even when the stock market goes up, sometimes it has to go down to get there.

I realize that's a lot of numbers I just threw at you. The most important takeaway from all of this historical data is that volatility is a buying opportunity, not something to run from.

Getting used to drawdowns

As an investor in the stock market, you have to get used to being in a state of drawdown. Going back to 1950, the S&P 500 has hit new all-time highs in just 7% of all trading days. If we invert, that means the stock market has been down from all-time highs 93% of the time. And you would have been down 10% or worse more than one-third of the time.

Table 12.1 shows how often the stock market experiences declines of different sizes.

Table 12.1: How often is the stock market down and by how much (S&P 500, 1950–2024)?

Drawdown From All-Time Highs	% of the time
Down 50% or Worse	0.1%
Down 40% or Worse	2.3%
Down 30% or Worse	5.4%
Down 20% or Worse	16.4%
Down 10% or Worse	36.1%
Down up to 10%	55.3%
All-Time Highs	7.0%

Source: YCharts.com.

If you're not comfortable sitting through losses, you're never going to make it in the stock market.

In the 20th century, we endured a pandemic, the Great Depression, two world wars, the Vietnam War, the Korean War, the Cold War, the Gulf War, 19 recessions, high inflation, low inflation, deflation, high rates, low rates, Black Monday, a handful of stock market crashes and dozens of corrections along the way.

In the 21st century (so far), we endured 9/11, the Iraq war, the war in Afghanistan, the pandemic, the Great Financial Crisis, the highest inflation in 40 years, negative oil prices, a lost decade in the stock market bookended by separate 50% crashes and a handful of recessions.

I could keep going. History is littered with unspeakable tragedies and yet we as a species somehow forge ahead. We create. We innovate. We grow. We make more money. Life goes on. Things eventually get better. Despite all of the nasty stuff that occurred the stock market was up 10% per year. Can I guarantee this will continue? Of course not. Does that mean you should abandon the stock market? I hope not.

Short-term vs. long-term volatility

In Wall Street parlance, volatility is considered risk. And the way finance people define risk is through mathematical formulas. For volatility, they calculate the standard deviation of returns. You might be a little rusty on statistics so allow me to explain.

Imagine you have a classroom full of students and measure everyone's height. Some of those students will be taller, some will be shorter and some will be close to average. Standard deviation is how much the student heights vary around the average. If the range is wide – spanning from Yao Ming (7'6") to Muggsy Bogues (5'3") – the standard deviation will be relatively high. Conversely, if most heights cluster closely around the average, the standard deviation will be lower. That's volatility.

The stock market has a rather high standard deviation. The returns are all over the place from year to year. On the other hand, bonds and cash are asset classes associated with relatively low volatility. They have lower highs and lower lows than the stock market.

However, this doesn't tell the whole story.

Volatility depends on your time frame. In the short run, bonds and cash can provide a buffer against volatility. Assuming you need to spend down part of your portfolio, rebalance into the pain, or desire an emotional hedge against the stock market, the lack of volatility in bonds and cash is a huge benefit.

Stocks can be insanely volatile in the short run, but in the long run, the volatility of stock returns falls considerably. Figure 12.6 shows the standard deviation of monthly returns for stocks, bonds and cash over various time frames.

Figure 12.6: Asset class volatility by holding period (S&P 500, 5-year Treasuries, 1-month T-bills, 1926–2024)

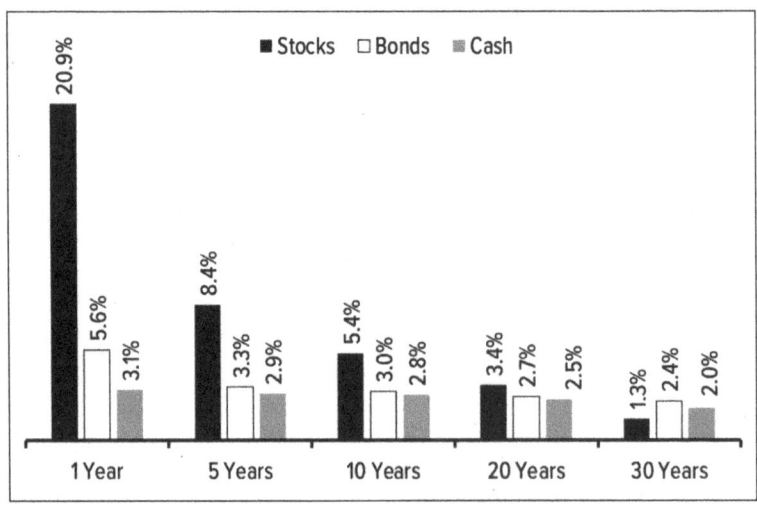

Source: Returns 2.0.

You can see that stock market volatility is much higher over rolling one-year returns. The best 12-month return for the S&P 500 over this period was 163%. The worst 12-month return was -68%. This range from high to low is wide enough to drive 17 cement trucks through. But the variance of returns narrows considerably as you extend the time horizon. Incredibly, stock market returns are less volatile than bonds and cash over a 30-year time frame! Stocks are always at risk of a drawdown or crash, but the variability in your returns goes down the longer you hold them.

To bring this discussion full circle, Roger Federer experienced plenty of volatility in the short run. He lost a lot of points in his matches. But the range of outcomes decreased the further out you extend his tennis matches. Federer's winning percentage for games (58%) was higher than his winning percentage for points (54%). He won more sets (76%) than games and more matches (82%) than sets.

Historical information like this can help put things into perspective, but historical data is rarely enough to help you sleep at night or change your behavior. Market averages tell a story, but no one's experience in the markets is ever average in the moment. The past is easy because we know what happened, but the future is messy since the uncertainty of the potential outcomes cannot be reduced.

If you need liquidity in the short term for spending purposes, that money shouldn't be invested in the stock market. If you have a time horizon measured in years and decades as opposed to days and months, the stock market makes more sense. Your mix of long-term and short-term assets depends on your ability to withstand losses with equanimity and your desire to sleep soundly at night. Every financial decision you make is a series of trade-offs and investing is no different in that regard.

Volatility is only a risk if it causes you to overreact and make unnecessary mistakes. One of the reasons the stock market provides such lovely returns in the long run is because it can be so darn confusing in the short run. You don't get the gains without living through the losses.

Every correction feels like it will never end while you are in it and with the benefit of hindsight always looks like a buying opportunity. No one ever said investing was easy. That's why the stock market offers you a risk premium – it's risky!

At least in the short term.

You don't get the result shown in Figure 12.7...

Figure 12.7: S&P 500 performance, 1950–2024

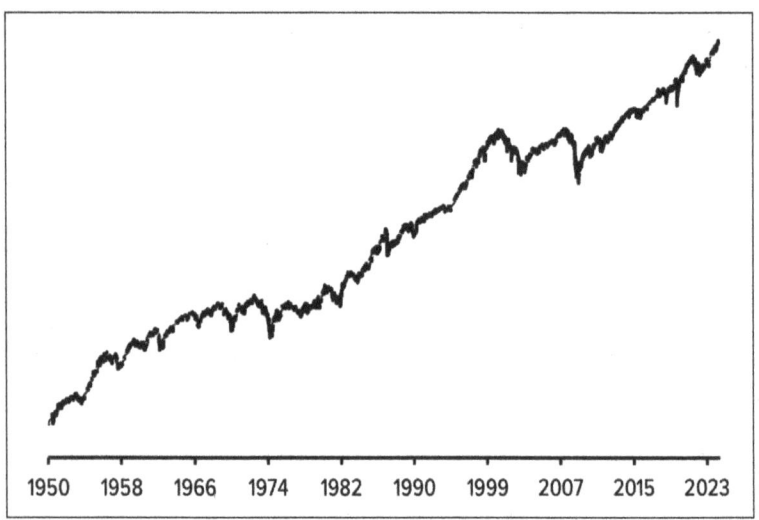

Source: YCharts.com.

...without living through the drawdowns shown in Figure 12.8.

Figure 12.8: S&P 500 drawdowns, 1950–2024

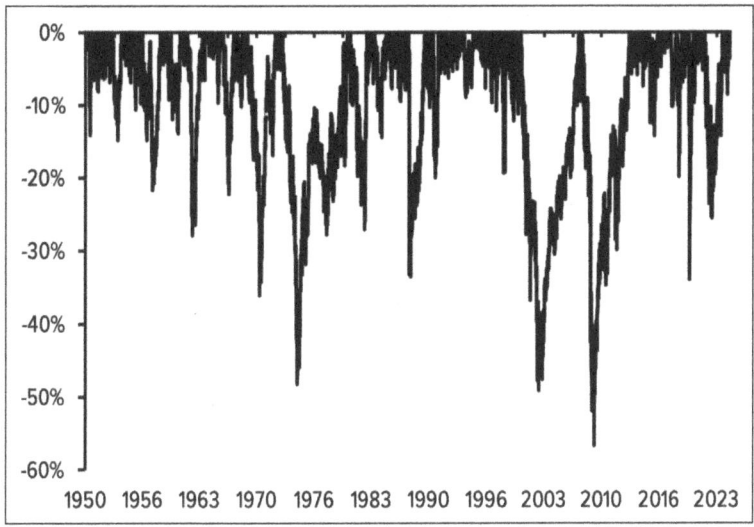

Source: YCharts.com.

Now let's take a look at how the cycle of fear and greed can play tricks with your emotions as an investor.

13.

THE DEATH OF EQUITIES

"Men resist randomness,
markets resist prophecy."

—MAGGIE MAHAR

AMAZON WENT PUBLIC in the spring of 1997.
That first year the stock was up more than 150%. The following year it gained close to 1,000%, and then another 40% and change in 1999 as the dot-com bubble really took off. The stock was down 80% in 2000 after the dot-com bubble burst. It would drop nearly 95% before all was said and done.

Amazon is now a trillion-dollar corporation and it seems so obvious it would become one of the most important companies in almost all of our lives. I break down more Amazon boxes in my garage every year than a UPS store. But it wasn't quite so obvious at the time when Amazon was still finding its way.

A few months before Amazon's IPO, Jeff Bezos flew to Boston to give a presentation at Harvard Business School. After giving a talk to a class, Bezos stood off to the side as the graduate students pretended he wasn't there to dissect the prospects of the online retailer. The consensus from the future Harvard MBAs was that Amazon probably wouldn't survive when other retailers made the move online. One student flatly told Bezos, "You seem like a really nice guy, so don't take this the wrong way, but you really need to sell to Barnes & Noble and get out now."*

Whoops.

Yogi Berra said it best when it comes to forecasting: "It's tough to make predictions, especially about the future."

Of course it is. The future is unknowable! The past is littered with terrible predictions about what will happen next.

In the early 1900s, a banker advised Henry Ford's lawyer to avoid investing in Ford Motor because "The horse is here to stay but the automobile is only a novelty – a fad."

In 1946 a Hollywood producer was positive the television would also become a fad when he said, "Television won't be able to hold on to any market it captures after the first six months. People will soon get tired of staring at a plywood box every night."

When Microsoft CEO Steve Ballmer was asked what his first reaction was when the iPhone was introduced in 2007, he laughed heartily and told a reporter it was too expensive and wouldn't appeal to business customers because it didn't have a keyboard.

Before their 1984 title fight in Russia, Ivan Drago told Rocky Balboa, "I will crush you" in the boxing ring. Rocky knocked out the Russian in the 15th round in a major upset. OK, that one is from *Rocky IV*, but you get the picture.

People aren't very good at making predictions about the stock market either.

---

* Bezos responded to the class by saying, "You might be right, but I think you might be underestimating the degree to which established brick-and-mortar business, or any company that might be used to doing things a certain way, will find it hard to be nimble or to focus attention on a new channel. I guess we'll see."

How many people own stocks?

The boom-bust nature of stock market cycles along with changes in household ownership in the market can help provide some context behind investor behavior in stocks.

Recall that just 2–3% of U.S. households owned stocks heading into the gigantic 1929 to 1932 market crash during the Great Depression. Most people still weren't all that interested in the market mainly because most households didn't have much in the way of disposable income to invest. In 1929, nearly 60% of American families had incomes that placed them below the poverty line.

The lost decades and economic stagnation that followed didn't do much to engender confidence in stocks as an asset class. That would all change in the post-Second World War era. The economic malaise following the Great Depression didn't really end until the Second World War kicked off a post-war recovery unlike anything the world had ever seen. The boom times following the war changed the trajectory of the United States and the rest of the world in terms of growth, jobs, income, demographics and wealth for decades to come.

The average pay for manufacturing workers was up almost 90% between 1939 and 1945. Disposable income for all Americans rose nearly 75% between 1929 and 1950. By 1945, GDP was 2.4 times the size of the economy in 1939. Frederick Lewis Allen called it "the most extraordinary increase in production that had ever been accomplished in five years in all economic history."

The middle class in America was more or less born of that post-Second World War era through a combination of a federal housing bill, a baby boom, and the large number of soldiers coming home from war looking to settle down and start a family. The number of new single-family homes built in America grew from 114,000 in 1944 to 1.7 million by 1950.

Once people owned homes and had some disposable income, they could finally consider investing some of their capital. It was still pretty slow going, though. In 1953 only 4% of the country owned stocks. Even after the 1950s bull market, which saw the U.S. stock market rise by nearly 500% – 19.5% per year for a decade – there were only 12.5 million stockholders out of a population of 177 million. Scars from the Great Depression cut deep.

By the 1960s, there were finally enough new investors who didn't wear the scars so stock ownership finally took off. Equity ownership reached 30% heading into the 1970s. It would fall to 15% by the end of that atrocious decade. You not only had stocks and bonds perform poorly in the 1970s, but savers could get double-digit yields on their cash in money markets, CDs and savings accounts. Why would you want to invest in stocks when you could earn 15% with no market risk?

That mentality led to the most infamous magazine cover in stock market history. In the summer of 1979 *BusinessWeek* published a cover story titled "The Death of Equities." Frankly, the timing could have been a little better. The stock market was about to embark on one of the greatest bull markets ever, as it rose 2,500%, or nearly 18% per year, from 1980 to 1999.

Sir John Templeton once opined, "Bull markets are born on pessimism, grow on skepticism, mature on optimism, and die on euphoria." It was fertile ground for a bull market heading into the 1980s because pessimism broke out to new all-time highs after the 1970s debacle. Barton Biggs once said, "A bull market is like sex. It feels best just before it ends." The opposite is true of a bear market – it feels the worst just before it ends. Inflation was still out of control. Stocks had gone nowhere for well over a decade. To combat seemingly never-ending inflation, the Fed raised interest rates to heights we've never seen before or since.

It made sense investors wanted nothing to do with the stock market. Here's an excerpt from the *BusinessWeek* article:

Further, this 'death of equity' can no longer be seen as something a stock market rally – however strong – will check.

It has persisted for more than 10 years through market rallies, business cycles, recession, recoveries, and booms. The public was first drawn to equities in big numbers in the 1950s by a massive promotion campaign by Wall Street that worked because the economic climate was right: fairly steady growth with little inflation. To bring equities back to life now, secular inflation would have to be wrung out of the economy, and then accounting policies would have to be made more realistic and tax laws rewritten. But these steps may not be enough.

The coming decades would see an explosion of equity ownership in America like never before. But investors weren't positioned for the coming bull market just yet.

Fidelity burst onto the fund scene in the 1960s as mutual funds became the new preferred way to invest in stocks during the Go-Go Years. The fund firm had $5 billion in assets in 1968 with 90% of the money invested in stocks. By 1982, it was managing $17 billion, but just 12% of assets were now in stocks. In the 20 years prior to the 1970s, pension plans kept more than half of their assets in the stock market. By 1982, they were putting just 24% into equities. "The Death of Equities" cover story was based on the reality at the time. Investors *were* abandoning stocks. But it wouldn't last.

Not only did interest rates and inflation peak in the early 1980s, but a tax bill in 1981 contained a provision that allowed workers to lower their taxable income by $2,000 a year if they put it into a new tax-deferred retirement account. The Individual Retirement Account (IRA) was born, and all that cash on the sidelines had a new home that allowed people to invest in stocks for the long run in a tax-deferred investment vehicle. Game on.

Fidelity was opening up 10,000 new accounts a day in the lead-up to the 1983 tax deadline. T. Rowe Price said 70% of incoming IRA money went into stock funds in 1983 versus just 28% in 1982. Merrill Lynch customers who opened accounts to invest in stocks doubled once IRAs became available. IRAs not only gave people an incentive to save for retirement but also forced them to realize they were on their own when it came to saving for their post-work years.

By 1987, 55 million people had opened a mutual fund account, and most of those funds were invested in stocks. The 1980s bull market was the first in history to include younger investors and the middle class. It helped that the eldest baby boomers were entering their prime earning years. The addition of low-cost brokerages and 401k accounts played a role here too. The stars were aligned. Then came a massive bubble.

The dot-com bubble wrecked a lot of portfolios once it deflated, but it got people interested and invested in the stock market in a big way. By the early 1980s, the share of households with a stake in the stock market was just 19%. The number of people who were invested in the stock market shot up to an estimated 60% of households by 2000. Almost two-thirds of those who owned stocks had purchased their first share after 1990. One-third of equity owners had made their first purchase after 1995.[*]

No one thought that scenario was possible coming out of the 1970s, save for one group of investors. Here's one more passage from "The Death of Equities" story:

> The problem is not merely that there are seven million fewer shareholders than there were in 1970. Younger investors, in particular, are avoiding stocks. Between 1970 and 1975, the number of investors declined in every age group but one: individuals 65 and older. While the number of investors under 65 dropped by about 25%, the number of investors over 65 jumped by more than 30%. **Only the elderly who have not**

---

[*] It was investors of all shapes and sizes too. In 1983, households with incomes of $250,000 or more owned 43% of all publicly traded stocks. By 1992, that share had dropped to 23%, while Americans with incomes of less than $75,000 saw their share jump from 24% in 1983 to 42% by 1992.

understood the changes in the nation's financial markets, or who are unable to adjust to them, are sticking with stocks.

Older investors holding onto or adding to their equity holdings were being openly mocked. Those silly long-term investors. Surely, the young and inexperienced investors throwing in the towel knew what they were doing... right?

Those 65 and over investors had lived through some cycles in their day. They knew lost decades were part of the bargain when it comes to investing in stocks. It was the young investors who broke the number one rule of compounding by interrupting it unnecessarily.

Here are some takeaways from this history lesson:

The best time to buy stocks is when they're out of favor. In the fall of 2008, a colleague confided in me that he was changing his 401k contributions from stocks to a stable value fund. He urged me to do the same as the entire financial system seemingly crumbled around us. This made no sense then or now. I was in my 20s at the time.*

Why would I run from the stock market when prices were lower than at any point in my working life? If the financial system ever implodes, does it matter what you invest in? At that point, canned food and ammo are better hedges than stocks and bonds.

As long as you have a long time horizon and money to invest, you should become more excited about the stock market the more others hate it.

There is a lifecycle of wealth. The problem with looking at the markets from the vantage point of static start and end points is that it's simply not realistic for the vast majority of investors. How many investors put their money in at one point in time and just leave it be? And how many investors do so at the precise top or bottom of the market?

---

* The retirement contributions I made throughout 2008 and early 2009 into the stock market will be the best investments I ever make.

Unless you're the heir to a wealthy fortune, you don't invest a single lump sum and let it ride. You invest your money periodically out of a regular paycheck, thus diversifying across time and market environment. If you're done saving, you're taking withdrawals, reinvesting income and dividends, rebalancing your portfolio or changing your asset allocation.

And the best part about investing on a set interval – quarterly, monthly, weekly, etc. – is that you diversify your entry points. You don't have to worry as much about tops and bottoms. Some purchases will be better than others, but so it goes. Dollar-cost averaging is far from the perfect investment strategy. The good news is you don't need to be perfect to find investment success. You just have to be consistent. That consistency matters most during down markets.

Risk is for the young. Your biggest assets as a young investor are time and human capital (your future earning potential). It's nearly impossible for young people to invest their money too aggressively in stocks. If stocks rise, the value of your portfolio increases. If stocks fall, you can invest your future savings at lower prices. Win-win.

Any investor who dutifully purchased stocks throughout the horrific 1970s market would not have felt great by the end of that decade, but they had set themselves up wonderfully for the years ahead. Let's say you put $100/month into the U.S. stock market throughout the 1970s. By the end of the decade, you would have contributed $12,000 in total, which would have grown to a little more than $15,000. That probably wouldn't feel great after a decade of investing. It was even worse after inflation.

But let's say you kept making those same contributions in the 1980s. Now we're up to $24,000 at cost, but the market value of your shares as of year-end 1989 would have been more than $90,000. All of those consistent purchases during the ups and downs of the 1970s paid off big time.

Bad returns are not always bad as long as you take advantage of them when they lead to good returns later. Your older self will thank you if you stay in the game when you're young.

The next chapter looks at why it's so important to think and act for the long term when it comes to compounding your capital.

14.

THE FIRST
RULE OF
COMPOUNDING

*"The big money is not in the buying
or the selling, but in the waiting."*

−CHARLIE MUNGER

T HERE'S AN ALLEGORY about a con artist who crafted high-end
chessboards for the rich.

His favorite mark was a wealthy king. The con artist had played
chess against the king many times and could tell his majesty wasn't
very good with numbers. But none of the king's underlings were brave
enough to tell the boss he wasn't good at math, so the ruler never
realized his deficiency.

The swindler crafted a scheme to exploit the king's vulnerability to
his advantage. He meticulously created the most exquisite chessboard
ever fashioned, each piece brimming with intricate details and
unmatched artistry. When the king laid eyes on this masterpiece, he
was thrilled. When asked how many gold coins or jewels it would
cost, the con artist replied, "I don't want your money. Just pay me in
grains of rice."

The king had plenty of rice throughout his lands, so he asked how much would be required.

"All I ask for is one grain of rice for the first square on the board, two for the second square, four for the third square, and so on. Just double the grains with each new square all the way up to the 64th space on the board."

Apparently, none of the king's staff had Microsoft Excel or a calculator, so no one bothered to do the math.

"I can handle a chessboard full of rice," the king said as he agreed to the deal.

The king told his servants to get the con artist his rice so he could enjoy his lovely new chessboard. Once they began to run the numbers, it was more challenging than initially thought. It only took until the 11th square to break 1,000 grains of rice. By the 21st square, the doubling of grains led to more than one million pieces of rice. In 20 more doubles from there they were up to one trillion grains. It would only get worse. The king couldn't possibly produce that much rice – it didn't exist. Of course, the con artist knew this and asked for gold or land in lieu of the rice.

Knowing he'd been duped, the king said he would be happy to pay up as soon as the con artist would individually count out the grains of rice he was owed.

Touche.

As Kenny Rogers once said, "You've gotta know when to hold 'em, know when to fold 'em." The con artist told the king to keep the chessboard as a gift and went on his merry way. You win some, you lose some.

Like the king, our brains are hardwired to think linearly, not exponentially. Unfortunately, in the real world, your returns from investing don't happen as quickly as the grains of rice multiplying on that chessboard. It takes time, and it requires patience and discipline to see a payoff. But if you wait long enough that payoff can be spectacular. A good chunk of investing is putting your money to work in the stock market and then waiting. You just have to ensure you don't screw things up along the way.

As Charlie Munger once said, "The first rule of compounding: Never interrupt it unnecessarily."

The eighth wonder of the world

Compounding might be the eighth wonder of the world, but it takes time to morph from a caterpillar into a butterfly. From 1950 to 2024, the S&P 500 was up 11.5% per year. Let's say you put $10,000 into the S&P at the outset of that 75-year period.

By 1960 your $10,000 would have grown to almost $60,000. By 1970 that $60,000 would double to more than $120,000, then $220,000 heading into the 1980s. Slow but steady growth. The original $10,000 would hit $1 million for the first time in 1989. Through the end of 2024, $10,000 invested in 1950 would have turned into $36 million! The snowball is tiny at first, but once it gets rolling the growth in undeniable.

The same is true when you average into the market over time. Let's assume you invest $10,000 at the start of every year for 30 years and earn 10% on your money. By the end of 30 years, you would have saved a grand total of $300,000, which would have grown to just shy of $1.7 million. Not bad. However, because of the way compounding works, the majority of the growth is back-loaded. In this simple example, your investment gains would take 14 years to outpace the amount you saved each year. Saving matters more than investing when you're just starting out. The total investment gains earned in this example are just shy of $1.4 million. However, nearly 60% of those profits come in the last six years. Compounding is back-loaded, so it takes perseverance.

The reason compounding is so back-loaded is the fact that it takes time for the snowball to build once it starts going downhill. In the early years of investing when you have a smaller balance, your investment returns earn you interest on your original contributions plus any small amount of accumulated interest or gains. In your later years you're earning interest on top of interest on top of interest and so on. If you compound $10,000 by 10% per year your annual return on investment would be $1,000 in the first year, more than $2,100 by the 10th year, $5,560 by year 20 and nearly $15,000 after 30 years of growth.

The problem is that it's easier for your brain to understand linear growth as opposed to exponential growth. Walking up the stairs is linear growth. Each step is the same height. In most houses, that's around seven inches. If you took 10 steps, it's pretty easy to calculate how many inches up you are (7+7+7+7+7+7+7+7+7+7). Now let's say you wanted to double the size of your stairs with every step. The first step would still be seven inches, the second 14", the third 28". At first it doesn't feel that different. But by the 10th step, the rise alone would be over 30 feet high – taller than a three-story building. That's compounding. Plus, there is the fact that you will be saving and investing more money as time goes on. It's gains on top of gains on top of a bigger pile of money.

The hard part about investing in the real world is life does not work like an Excel spreadsheet. You cannot input your expected returns into a financial model and assume you'll earn that number year in and year out. The stock market doesn't work like that. Compounding in a retirement calculator is neat and tidy. Compounding in the stock market is messy and lumpy.

Stock market returns are lumpy

Investing in the stock market would be far easier if you could simply bank on 10% each and every year. Unfortunately, it doesn't work that way. There would be no risk if stock market returns were consistent each year. If there were no risk, the stock market wouldn't offer such attractive returns. It's the catch-22 of investing in risk assets.

If you want consistency over the long haul, you have to accept lower returns. And if you want higher returns over the long haul, you have to accept more volatility. You can never truly escape risk; you just change how you accept it.

The volatility of stocks is easily observable when looking at the year-to-year returns on the U.S. stock market, as shown in Figure 14.1.

Figure 14.1: S&P 500 calendar year returns (1928–2024)

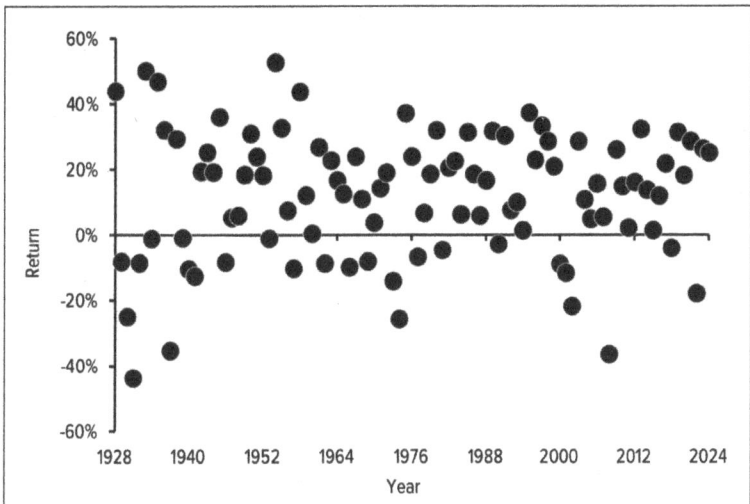

Source: NYU.

It's like the returns are on a yo-yo from one year to the next. You could have periods of multiple down years in a row (like 1929 to 1932) or a cluster of positive years in a row (like 1995 to 1999). There are more gains than losses but no rhyme or reason when it comes to annual stock market returns.

Figure 14.2 shows another way of viewing these calendar year returns; as you can see, annual stock market returns are anything but average.

Figure 14.2: Stock market return distribution: 1928–2024

-20% or worse	-20% to -10%	-10% to 0%	0% to 10%	10% to 20%	20% to 30%	30% or better
				19.2%		
				19.0%		
				18.8%	29.3%	52.6%
				18.5%	28.5%	50.0%
				18.5%	28.4%	46.7%
			10.0%	18.3%	28.3%	43.8%
		−1.1%	7.5%	18.2%	26.6%	43.7%
		−1.2%	7.4%	18.0%	26.1%	37.2%
		−1.2%	6.5%	16.5%	25.9%	37.0%
		−3.1%	6.2%	16.4%	25.1%	35.8%
		−4.2%	5.8%	15.9%	24.9%	33.1%
		−4.7%	5.7%	15.6%	23.8%	32.6%
		−7.0%	5.5%	14.8%	23.8%	32.2%
		−8.2%	5.2%	14.2%	23.7%	31.9%
−22.0%	−10.5%	−8.3%	4.8%	13.5%	22.7%	31.7%
−25.1%	−10.7%	−8.4%	3.6%	12.4%	22.6%	31.5%
−25.9%	−11.9%	−8.6%	2.1%	12.1%	22.3%	31.2%
−35.3%	−12.8%	−8.8%	1.4%	11.8%	21.6%	31.2%
−36.6%	−14.3%	−9.0%	1.3%	10.8%	20.9%	30.8%
−43.8%	−18.0%	−10.0%	0.3%	10.7%	20.4%	30.2%

Source: NYU.

One of the strangest aspects of stock market returns in any given year is how seldom they finish around the long-term average. Over the 97 years from 1928 to 2024, there were just three years in which returns finished in the 9% to 11% range. There is a lot of variation around the 10% long-run average.

Breaking things down a little further for calendar year returns from 1928 to 2024:

- 71 out of 97 years saw positive returns (73% of the time).
- 26 out of 97 years saw negative returns (27% of the time).
- 68 out of 97 years were double-digit gains or losses (70% of the time).
- 56 out of 97 years were double-digit gains (58% of the time).
- 12 out of 97 years were double-digit losses (12% of the time).
- 42 out of 97 years were gains or losses of 20% or more (43% of the time).
- 36 out of 97 years were gains of 20% or more (37% of the time).
- 6 out of 97 years were losses of 20% or worse (6% of the time).

Not only have stocks been up roughly three out of every four years on average, but they've shown double-digit gains or losses on a similar frequency. The stock market has finished the year with double-digit gains roughly six out of every 10 years. In contrast, it's more like one out of every eight years for a double-digit loss. Nearly 40% of all years have seen a gain of 20% or more! Historically, **you would have been more likely to experience a 20% gain than a down year in the stock market**.

How you view the stock market also depends on your time horizon.

32 years of stock market returns

Figure 14.3 offers a different way to look at returns over various time horizons for the S&P 500 going back to 1993.

Figure 14.3: Calendar-year annualized forward S&P 500 returns

Starting Year

# Years Forward	1993	1994	1995	1996	1997	1998	1999	2000	2001	2002	2003	2004	2005	2006	2007	2008
1	10%	1%	38%	23%	33%	29%	21%	-9%	-12%	-22%	29%	11%	5%	16%	6%	-37%
2	6%	18%	30%	28%	31%	25%	5%	-11%	-17%	0%	19%	8%	10%	11%	-18%	-11%
3	15%	20%	31%	28%	28%	12%	-1%	-15%	-4%	4%	14%	10%	9%	-8%	-6%	-3%
4	17%	23%	30%	26%	17%	6%	-7%	-5%	-1%	4%	15%	9%	-5%	-1%	-1%	-2%
5	20%	24%	29%	18%	11%	-1%	-1%	-2%	1%	6%	13%	-2%	0%	2%	0%	2%
6	22%	24%	21%	13%	4%	4%	1%	-1%	3%	6%	2%	2%	3%	2%	2%	6%
7	22%	18%	16%	7%	8%	5%	2%	1%	3%	-2%	6%	4%	3%	4%	6%	7%
8	17%	14%	10%	9%	8%	5%	3%	2%	-3%	2%	7%	4%	4%	7%	7%	7%
9	14%	9%	12%	10%	8%	6%	4%	-4%	0%	3%	6%	5%	7%	8%	6%	7%
10	9%	11%	12%	9%	8%	6%	-1%	-1%	1%	3%	7%	7%	8%	7%	7%	8%
11	11%	11%	11%	10%	8%	1%	1%	0%	1%	4%	9%	8%	7%	8%	8%	7%
12	11%	11%	12%	9%	3%	3%	2%	1%	3%	6%	10%	7%	7%	9%	7%	9%
13	10%	11%	11%	5%	5%	4%	2%	2%	5%	7%	9%	8%	9%	8%	9%	10%
14	11%	11%	7%	6%	6%	4%	3%	4%	5%	6%	9%	9%	8%	9%	9%	11%
15	10%	6%	8%	7%	5%	4%	5%	4%	5%	7%	10%	8%	9%	10%	11%	9%
16	7%	8%	8%	6%	6%	6%	5%	4%	5%	8%	9%	9%	10%	11%	9%	10%
17	8%	8%	8%	7%	7%	6%	5%	5%	6%	7%	10%	10%	11%	9%	10%	11%
18	8%	8%	9%	8%	8%	6%	5%	5%	6%	8%	11%	11%	9%	10%	10%	
19	8%	8%	10%	9%	7%	6%	6%	5%	7%	9%	11%	9%	10%	11%		
20	8%	9%	10%	8%	8%	7%	6%	6%	7%	10%	10%	10%	10%			
21	9%	9%	9%	8%	8%	7%	7%	7%	8%	8%	11%	10%				
22	9%	9%	10%	9%	8%	8%	7%	8%	7%	9%	11%					
23	9%	9%	10%	8%	9%	8%	8%	6%	8%	9%						
24	9%	10%	9%	9%	9%	9%	7%	7%	8%							
25	10%	9%	10%	10%	10%	8%	8%	8%								
26	9%	10%	11%	10%	9%	8%	8%									
27	10%	10%	11%	9%	9%	9%										
28	10%	11%	10%	10%	10%											
29	11%	10%	10%	10%												
30	10%	10%	11%													
31	10%	11%														
32	11%															

Source: Returns 2.0.

Starting Year

2009	2010	2011	2012	2013	2014	2015	2016	2017	2018	2019	2020	2021	2022	2023	2024
26%	15%	2%	16%	32%	14%	1%	12%	22%	-4%	31%	18%	29%	-18%	26%	25%
21%	8%	9%	24%	23%	7%	7%	17%	8%	12%	25%	23%	3%	2%	26%	
14%	11%	16%	20%	15%	9%	11%	9%	15%	14%	26%	8%	10%	9%		
15%	16%	16%	15%	14%	12%	7%	14%	16%	18%	13%	12%	14%			
18%	15%	13%	15%	16%	8%	12%	15%	18%	9%	16%	15%				
17%	13%	12%	16%	12%	12%	13%	17%	11%	12%	17%					
15%	13%	14%	13%	15%	13%	15%	11%	13%	14%						
14%	14%	11%	15%	15%	15%	10%	13%	15%							
15%	12%	13%	15%	17%	11%	12%	14%								
13%	14%	14%	17%	13%	12%	13%									
15%	14%	15%	13%	14%	13%										
15%	15%	12%	14%	15%											
16%	12%	13%	15%												
13%	13%	14%													
14%	14%														
15%															

Here's how to read this chart: Pick a starting year. Then, go down the number of years on the left-hand side and the corresponding square will tell you the annualized return from that starting point. For example, the nine-year annual return starting in 1993 was 14% per year. The 16-year annual return from 2005 was 10% per year.

I also highlighted the negative returns on the chart. There were far more positive returns than negative, but there were some painful periods for investors over this time. There were no losses going out 11 years or more, but starting in 1999 or 2000 led to a lost decade. You also had multiple instances of losses going out two, three, four and five years into the future. Five years can feel like an eternity when your investments aren't earning you anything.

The range of outcomes is also interesting to consider. The 10-year annual returns ranged from -1% to 17% per year. Over 15 years there was a high of 14% per year compared to a low of just 4%. On a five-year time horizon the range was -2% to 29% annualized. Your experience in the stock market can vary drastically depending on your timing and your start or end point.

The good news is that the long-term removes a lot of variation from the equation. Look at the returns in the bottom left – they're all in a fairly tight range. The 32-year annual return for the S&P 500 from 1993 to 2024 was 11% per year. In that time frame, we experienced an emerging markets currency crisis in 1998, the Long-Term Capital Management blow-up, the dot-com bubble, 9/11, the housing bubble, the Great Financial Crisis, the European Debt Crisis, the pandemic, the highest inflationary spike in four decades, and much more.

In bad years when everything is going down, you'll always wish you would've taken less risk. In good years when everything is going up, you'll always wish you would've taken more risk.

The important point here is that a longer time horizon is your friend as an investor. There will always be volatility over the short term. You could even experience godawful returns over a decade. But when you have a multi-decade time horizon, the compounding you experience in the stock market can be incredible.

Unfortunately for investors, it's never been easier to pay such close attention to the short-term movements of the stock market. That makes the benefits even greater for those who can ignore the short term to focus on the long term.

Compounding is for patient people.

Now let's turn our attention to the biggest bubble in history to show how the stock market can test your patience.

15.

THE BIGGEST BUBBLE EVER

"Nothing obscures your financial
judgment on investments more than the
sight of your neighbor getting rich."

—JP MORGAN

NUI ONOUE WAS raised in a small village in Japan where she lived a life of poverty.

After moving to Osaka, Japan's second-largest city, as a young woman she worked in a bar as a hostess, serving drinks to wealthy businessmen. Onoue worked her way up and by the time she was in her mid-30s, she owned her own restaurant and mahjong parlor. For decades, she ran her restaurants without drawing much attention to herself.

By the end of the 1980s, this obscure restaurant owner would become the largest individual stock market investor in all of Japan, which by then was the largest stock market in the world. This woman who had no finance ties whatsoever was worth more than Warren Buffett (on paper). At one point, Onoue owned some $800 million worth of shares in just 20 stocks. She claimed to receive stock tips straight from God

Almighty. Her brokers were required to attend weekly Buddhist prayer sessions if they wanted her business and they obliged. Those stock tips from a higher power worked wonders when the Japanese stock market rocketed higher throughout the 1980s. Unfortunately, she didn't get a heads-up from a higher power before the bubble popped.

J. Paul Getty once said, "If you owe the bank $100, that's your problem. If you owe the bank $100 million, that's the bank's problem." When the Japanese stock market blew up, the diminutive restaurant owner was the bank's problem.

Onoue was in debt to the tune of $3 *billion* to a handful of Japan's biggest banks. She was later charged with fraud for using $2.5 billion-worth of forged certificates of deposits as collateral to buy stocks on margin. In short order, Onoue went from being the biggest individual shareholder in Japan to the largest individual debtor in the country once she filed for bankruptcy.

The mania in Japan during the latter half of the 1980s was so insane the banks or the brokers didn't bat an eyelid at lending billions of dollars to a restaurant owner who claimed to receive stock picks from above. As long as the stock market was going up, no one cared. But stocks eventually stopped going up and it all came crashing down. Onoue was sentenced to 12 years in prison for fraud.

How is it possible that this small-time business owner secured billions of dollars in loans to buy stocks?

It was the biggest financial asset bubble in history, that's how.

With all due respect to tulip mania in the 1600s, the South Sea Bubble of the 1700s, the railway bubble of the 1800s, the Roaring Twenties and the internet bubble of the 1990s, nothing compares to the 1980s financial asset bubble in Japan.

It was uncharted territory, as Japan had never really experienced a financial bubble before. Remarkably, the country is home to over 33,000 businesses that are at least 100 years old – more than 40% of the world's total. Among them, more than 3,100 have lasted at least 200 years, and 140 have endured for over 500 years. This deep-rooted stability reflects a culture of patience and long-term thinking, a stark contrast to the United States, where economic bubbles seem to emerge every decade or so.

If we're judging purely by fundamentals alone, the biggest bubble in U.S. stock market history was the dot-com mania of the 1990s. After the S&P 500 rose nearly 650% from 1980 to 1994, the stock market ripped off consecutive gains of 37%, 23%, 33%, 28% and 21% from 1995 to 1999. The Nasdaq 100 was up an ungodly 817% in those same five years. That's annual returns of 55% *per year* for five years, which would have turned an initial $10,000 investment at the outset of 1995 into more than $91,000 by the end of 1999.

Every financial asset bubble in history starts out as a good idea that gets taken too far. The internet has given us everything and more that people were extrapolating back in the 1990s, but we had to go through the dot-com boom bust to get there. Things got silly in a hurry during the boom times. Newly listed tech companies were doubling and tripling the day they went public. Investors were clamoring for any company with .com in its name – business model, revenue or profits be damned. It was the height of euphoric behavior in the U.S. stock market as herd behavior replaced any semblance of rational analysis.

At the apex of the dot-com mania, the U.S. stock market would reach its highest valuations in history by the end of 1999. The stock market was trading at a multiple of almost 45x earnings compared to the long-term average of 17x. To put this number in perspective, the previous high at that point was 33x, which occurred at the stock market peak in September 1929, just before the Great Depression.[*]

After the dot-com bubble burst in the spring of 2000, the U.S. stock market was cut in half over the ensuing two-and-a-half-year bear market. It was the largest crash investors had experienced since

---

[*] Robert Shiller created the cyclically-adjusted price to earnings ratio (CAPE) to compare valuation measures across various market cycles using data going back to 1871. This is not a perfect valuation measure because the perfect valuation measure does not exist, but it can be useful for putting different markets into context.

the 1970s. The tech-heavy Nasdaq fell more than 80% and took nearly a decade-and-a-half to break even from those lows.

Despite the exuberance of the dot-com era, the valuations look tame compared to the peak of Japan's stock market bubble in 1989. Chart 15.1 shows the run-up to peak valuation levels for both Japanese stocks in the 1980s and U.S. stocks in the 1990s on the same scale.

Figure 15.1: Peak valuations: Japan in the 1980s vs. the dot-com bubble (CAPE ratio)

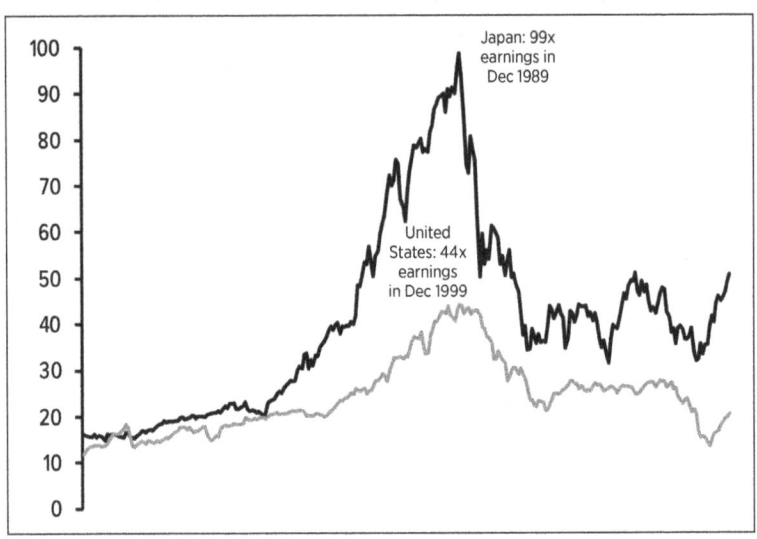

Source: Barclays.

By 1989, valuations for Japanese stocks were more than double the dot-com peak for the S&P 500 in 1999. You could say the dot-com bubble is not in the same ballpark as Japan's stock market bubble, but that's not going far enough. It's not even in the parking lot adjacent to the ballpark. Japan's stock prices were in a different stratosphere.

In the 1980s, share prices increased three times faster than corporate profits for Japanese corporations. Returns for Japanese equities were ludicrously high in the 1980s, and that was after they performed well in the 1970s. From 1970 to 1989, Japanese large-cap companies were up more than 22% per year, while Japanese small-cap stocks gained closer to 30% per year – for 20 years! A $100,000 investment in Japanese large-cap stocks in 1970 would have turned into more than $5 million by 1989. In small cap stocks over that same time frame, $100,000 would have grown to $19 million. A nation's stock market simply cannot grow at those rates for that long without causing major imbalances in the economy and financial sector.

Japan's financial situation was imbalanced to the nth degree.

The stock market in Japan went from 29% of GDP in 1980 to 151% by 1989. In 1980, Japan made up 15% of global equity markets by market capitalization. By 1989 it represented closer to 45% of total world stock markets. And this happened while the U.S. stock market appreciated more than 17% per year! Japan was lapping the field.

By the end of the 1980s, everywhere you looked there were magazine cover stories about Japan overtaking the United States as the world's preeminent economic power. U.S. corporations were being pressured to adopt Japan's business practices. The market value of Japanese stocks was double that of American corporations, even though the United States had a GDP that was twice the size of Japan's economy. Japan had seven of the 10 largest banks in the world while the biggest bank – Nomura – had more capital at its disposal than the five largest banks in the U.S. combined.

The craziest thing is the stock market wasn't even the biggest financial asset bubble in Japan during the 1980s – it was the housing market.

A willful suspension of disbelief

Japan was the biggest asset bubble in history because it wasn't just a stock market bubble – it was an everything bubble. The housing market was even more overvalued as land speculation took off like an Apollo spacecraft.

Here are some crazy but true Japanese real estate facts and figures from the bubble times:

- From 1956 to 1986, land prices increased by 5,000% even though consumer prices only doubled in that time.
- By 1990, the total Japanese property market was valued at over 2,000 trillion yen, or roughly 4x the real estate value of the entire United States, despite the U.S. being 25x larger in terms of landmass and having 200 million more people.
- Tokyo itself was on equal footing with the U.S. in terms of real estate values.
- At the market peak, the grounds of Tokyo's Imperial Palace were estimated to be worth more than Canada's entire real estate market.
- The property market in Japan in 1989 was five times the size of Japan's economy.

A common trait every financial bubble shares is the deliberate suspension of disbelief, and the Japanese housing boom was no exception. People in Japan adopted a misguided mindset, believing they didn't need to worry about skyrocketing land values because land transactions are infrequent in the country. Both the public and government officials convinced themselves that the soaring land prices were illusory – an attitude that is a hallmark of financial manias.

Christopher Wood, the former editor of *The Economist* in Japan, wrote about how this suspension in disbelief played out in the Japanese housing market in his book, *The Bubble Economy*:

> For all its high-tech gadgetry and automated vending machines, Japan remains a feudal society at heart whose members, like peasants throughout the ages, believe in the value of land. Behind many a salaryman there is a grandfather or elderly relative still toiling in the fields. Their blue-suited salaried

offspring still count their net worth primarily as the dirt on which their prefabricated houses sit.

In Japan virtually all of the value of a property lies in the land, not the building. As a result, buildings are knocked down and replaced with almost reckless abandon.

I guess since they valued the land so much more than the buildings the assumption was the actual price of the land didn't matter.

The problem with this mindset was the sheer number of individuals and financial institutions that received loans backed by land with sharply rising values. Banks issued these loans, insurance companies invested in the bonds tied to them, and households borrowed against their inflated value. Expecting people to overlook the fact that their paper wealth had soared was delusional.

It's irrelevant whether properties are rarely sold. A stock market mania can create a wealth effect that influences corporate behavior and household risk-taking. A housing boom affects even more parts of the economy – banks, loan officers, construction, households, institutional investors, and more. It's nearly impossible to prevent the ripple effects from spreading throughout the economy.

Charles Kindleberger referred to the Japanese bubble economy as a "perpetual motion machine." Higher real estate prices led to higher stock prices which led to more capital available for lending at the Japanese banks.

In 1979, consumer debt in Japan was nine trillion yen. By 1991, it had increased sevenfold to 67 trillion yen. Wealthy Japanese business tycoons began borrowing against their real estate holdings to purchase vast art collections. One Japanese collector doubled the previous record for sales of Van Gogh and Renoir paintings. More than 160 golf courses were built in Japan between 1989 and 1991. There were another 1,200 under construction or in the approval process that never got completed once the bubble burst. The price of the golf memberships traded like stocks. There were over 20 golf clubs that cost more than $1 million to join. At the peak of the euphoria, Japan's 1,700 golf courses were estimated to have a total membership market value of some $200 billion.

Of course, Isaac Newton's theory of gravity showed up in Japan eventually. Japan's central banks had seen enough and began raising interest rates to slow the speculation. They set out to prick the bubble and did they ever. Interest rates doubled between early 1989 and late 1990, which finally stopped the mania in its tracks. The perpetual motion machine then began to unwind.

Quantitative investment pioneer Cliff Asness once remarked, "The term bubble should indicate a price that no reasonable future outcome can justify." By the late 1980s, valuations in both Japanese stocks and real estate had soared to such extreme heights that no conceivable future outcome could justify them.

Thirty-five years later, housing prices in Japan were still more than 40% below where they were at the peak of the bubble in 1989 on an inflation-adjusted basis, as shown in Figure 15.2.

Figure 15.2: Real housing prices in Japan (1975–2024)

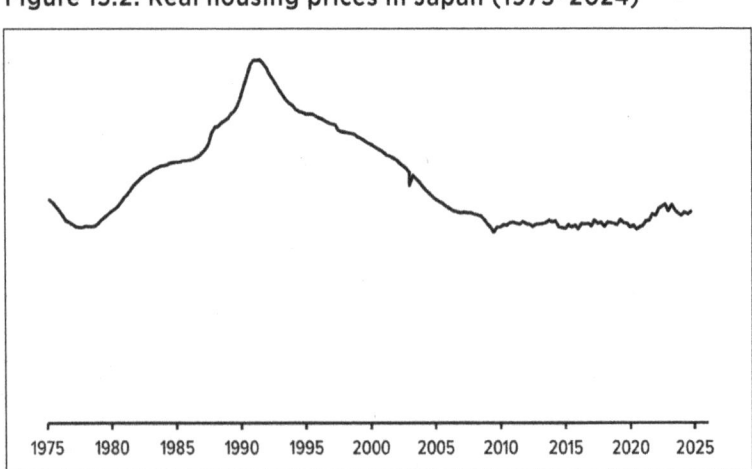

Source: Dallas Federal Reserve.

From 1970 to 1989, the worst drawdown for the Nikkei 225 index of Japanese stocks was -37%. Once the bubble burst, the Nikkei fell nearly 50% in the first nine months of 1990 alone. By 1993, the market was down almost 60%. As bad as those losses were, the worst part about it wasn't necessarily the magnitude of the crash but the length of time over which it occurred. There have been lost decades, singular, in the U.S. stock market. Japanese stock market investors experienced back-to-back-to-back lost decades.

The Nikkei didn't technically bottom until the end of the Great Financial Crisis in early-2009, a full 20 years after the peak! At that point, the Japanese stock market was down more than 80% from the 1989 highs. The stock market finally started going up in the 2010s, but remained underwater from the 1989 highs until new all-time highs were finally reached in 2024.

On a total return basis, which includes dividends reinvested, the MSCI Japan Index was up a grand total of 63% from 1990 to 2024. That's an annual return of 1.4% per year. You would have been better off investing in bonds or T-bills for three-and-a-half decades than investing in Japanese stocks at the peak in 1990, with much less volatility to boot. By 2024, Japan's stock market was just 6% of world stock market capitalization, down from the peak of 45% in 1989. Japan was all risk with little-to-no reward for three-and-a-half decades.

This is why *Now show Japan* exists. An entire generation of stock market investors in one of the biggest developed economies in the world experienced dreadful, terrible, no-good returns over the long run.

Japan was such a money loser for investors for so long that it disproves the idea of stocks for the long run, right? How could you possibly believe in buy-and-hold when a situation like this has played out?

I still believe!

Long live buy and hold!

In the next chapter, I'm going to put *Now Show Japan* into perspective and provide some context around how to think about the long run when investing in the stock market. As you'll see, the Japan story is the very reason why it's so important to think and act for the long term when it comes to compounding your capital.

16.

NOW SHOW
JAPAN

"Everything ends badly, otherwise
is wouldn't end."

—BRIAN FLANAGAN

I N 1955, DR. HENRY BEECHER published a research paper
demonstrating that "the placebo can have a powerful
therapeutic effect."

Beecher investigated the impact of the placebo effect on patients
with various health issues. His findings revealed that giving a placebo
medication improved pain management in 30–40% of patients
suffering from injuries, asthma, high blood pressure, and even
heart attacks.

Placebos are like using blanks in a gun – they have no actual,
physical effect whatsoever. The theory behind the placebo effect is that
it's all psychological. You tell the patient there is a medication that can
help, and the power of belief makes them feel better. Placebos sound
good in theory, but we humans are complex creatures.

Most doctors have remained skeptical about the effectiveness
of placebos. But what does the scientific evidence say? In the 21st

century, two doctors set out to test Beecher's theory through a series of clinical trials. Their research found minimal evidence that placebos provided any pain relief for patients in need. They concluded, "There is no justification for the use of placebos." Published in 2001, their findings have remained unchallenged, leading to the conclusion that the placebo effect is not real.

So what's going on here? Why did everyone get fooled by the placebo effect for so many decades?

The most straightforward answer is a reversion to the mean.

Mean reversion is the idea that outlier events or values are likely to revert back to their average levels over time. In other words, if a variable is significantly above or below its average in one period, it will likely move closer to the average in the following periods.

In the case of placebos, the average state for most people is good health. Most individuals who are sick or in pain eventually recover as the body heals and fights off illnesses that naturally resolve over time. People often seek medical help when their pain or symptoms are at the worst. Although it might appear that a placebo helps people feel better, the more straightforward explanation is that most people naturally improve from their lowest point.

Nobel Prize-winning behavioral expert Daniel Kahneman was once asked to analyze the performance of pilots in the Israeli Air Force. Flight instructors were trying to improve their incentive systems to better motivate the pilots. They observed that after a pilot performed exceptionally well and received praise, their next flight was usually worse. Conversely, pilots who had a poor flight were reprimanded and then showed improvement in their following flight. This led to the conclusion that praise was detrimental to performance, while punishment led to better results. However, Kahneman approached the issue from a different perspective and realized that the changes in performance were not due to the instructors' feedback at all. They were simply a result of reversion to the mean.

Which brings us to Japan's stock market.

Japan's meanest of reversions

Just as the human body has a natural tendency to get sick and recover over time, financial markets also exhibit a similar pattern of self-correction. Whether it's health or wealth, what goes down often comes back up and vice versa – not because of a miracle cure or market wizardry, but due to the powerful force of mean reversion.

When the stock market gets sick, sometimes the illness is more severe than others, but it does tend to get better even when it looks to be on its deathbed. On the other hand, the boom times never last forever and are inevitably followed by a bust. Above-average performance eventually leads to below-average performance and vice versa.

The hard part is that mean reversion doesn't act on a set schedule. It's unpredictable in terms of both timing and magnitude. Trees don't grow to the sky, but it's nearly impossible to know when they're going to be cut in half because human nature is the wild card in the timing of these things.

Japan's stock market experienced the meanest of reversions, but I'm going to tell you a little secret – Japan's long-term returns are still pretty good.

Yes, it's true!

Japan's stock market *was* stagnant for over three decades, delivering putrid long-term returns following the bursting of the largest asset bubble in history. But what if we combine the boom and the bust to see the full cycle?

Figure 16.1 shows the annual returns during both the bull market and the bear market phases, along with the entire 55-year time frame.

Figure 16.1: Japan stock market returns (1970–2024)

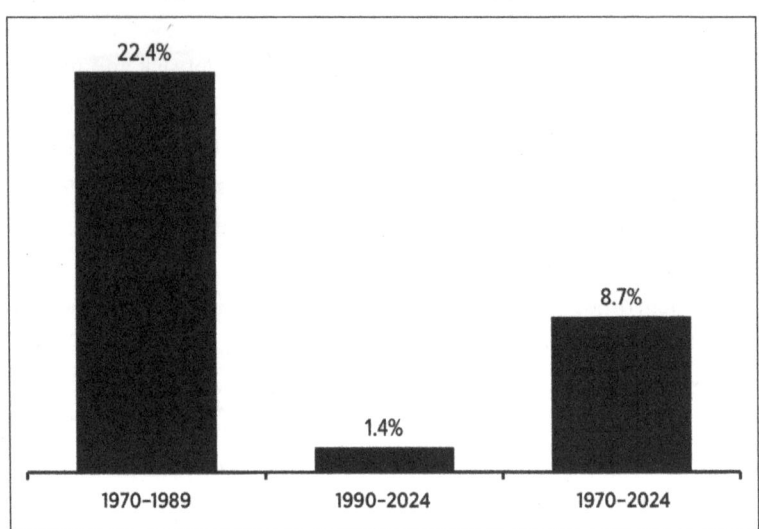

Source: MSCI Japan.

Over the long run, Japanese stocks are up nearly 9% per year. That's lower than the 11% return for the U.S. stock market in that time, but it's a respectable return over five-and-a-half decades.

Is this fun with numbers? In some ways, yes. You can win any argument you want about stock market history by changing your start and end dates. But who says 30 years is the definition of long term in the stock market? Over 50 years, Japanese stocks have done just fine. The problem is the 1980s bubble pulled forward decades of future returns as valuations went to Jupiter. Returns were so high in the 1970s and 1980s that you needed low returns in the ensuing decades to balance them out.

None of the *Now Show Japan* rebuttals to long-term buy-and-hold investing ever mention this. The Japanese stock market has worked over the long term. The returns were simply compressed in a short period of time and then experienced mean reversion to even things out.

The lesson of Japan's three-decade-long stock market malaise is not that long-term investing doesn't work. It does! Japan's lost decades teach us the importance of mean reversion. Valuations matter. Returns can't stay abnormally high forever. And when building a portfolio, it's important to avoid a single point of failure that can cause your investment performance to stagnate.

Avoiding a single point of failure

In 1995, Pixar Animation Studio was on a rocket ship of a growth trajectory. *Toy Story* came out in November to rave reviews and made more money than anyone thought possible. The first full-length animated film created entirely using computer-generated imagery (CGI) grossed over $360 million worldwide.

The Pixar team was riding high on their success, but Steve Jobs was already anticipating the company's first failure. He persuaded co-founder Ed Catmull that it was only a matter of time before Pixar released a film that bombed at the box office. To brace for this possibility, Jobs encouraged Pixar to go public so they could secure the funding needed to withstand a potential flop. Jobs argued that expanding Pixar's capital base would enable the company to fund its own projects and have greater control over its creative direction. More importantly, it would provide financial stability in case of a future failure. Jobs believed it was risky to rely solely on the success of each new release to sustain the company.

Catmull described his feelings about this idea in his excellent book, *Creativity Inc.*:

> The underlying logic of his reasoning shook me: We were going to screw up, it was inevitable. And we didn't know when or how. We had to prepare, then, for an unknown problem – a hidden problem. From that day on, I resolved to bring as many hidden problems as possible to light, a process that would require what might seem like an uncommon commitment to self-assessment.

Having a financial cushion would help us recover from failure, and Steve was right to secure one. But the more important goal for me was to try to remain vigilant, to always be on the lookout for signs that we were screwing up – without knowing, of course, when that would occur or how it might come to light.

Leaders often ask their team to perform a post-mortem to understand what went wrong after the fact. Jobs was asking for a pre-mortem to anticipate what could go wrong in advance, without knowing what the trigger would be.

The fundamental data from the past – earnings, revenues, cash flows, dividends, etc. – is the easy part of investing. Data is ubiquitous. You can map out historical risk factors with pinpoint accuracy, but figuring out where the future risks lie is at best a guessing game. The future is unknowable because unexpected events happen all the time, and no one knows when our collective emotions will take the markets too high or too low. There is no predicting when a bubble the size of the Grand Canyon will form like it did in Japan during the 1980s and thrust returns into outer space, just like there is no predicting when a crash of epic proportions will bring it back to earth.

Investor Josh Wolfe once said, "Failure comes from a failure to imagine failure." One of the best ways to manage these risks is to avoid having a single point of financial failure be your downfall. You do this in practice through diversification.

Exceptions to the rule

As the old saying goes, "The young man knows the rules, but the old man knows the exceptions."

Japan's dreadful three-decade-long returns don't invalidate the need to think and act for the long term. They simply remind you of the risks involved in concentrating your investments in any one strategy or region of the world. This is the first single point of failure to avoid: **avoid home country bias**.

Each year, Elroy Dimson, Paul Marsh and Mike Staunton publish the "Global Investment Returns Yearbook" that updates the performance numbers for developed economy stock markets from the start of the 20th century. It's over 100 years' worth of data, which is obviously longer than any individual's time horizon. However, looking at the long-run returns can provide valuable lessons for investors.

Figure 16.2 shows the inflation-adjusted annual returns for 21 different stock markets around the globe starting in the year 1900.

Figure 16.2: Inflation-adjusted returns by country (1900–2022)

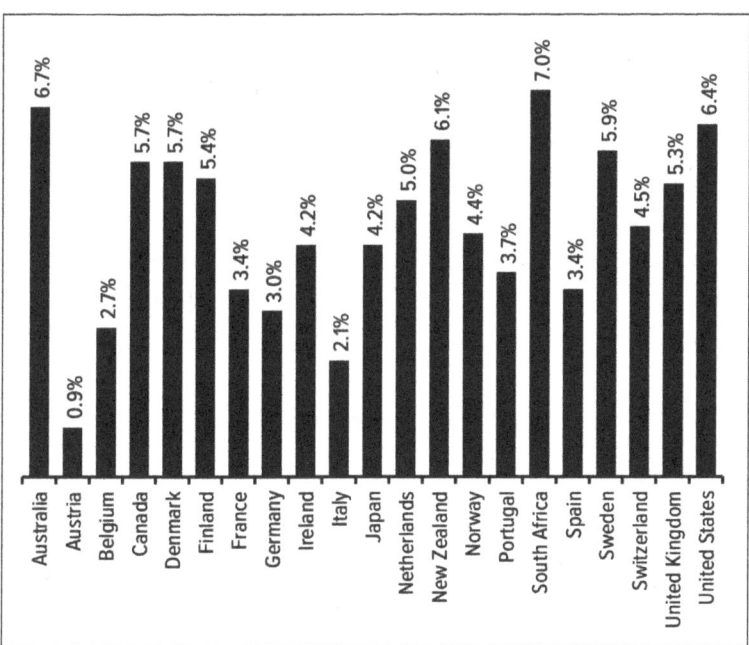

Source: Dimson, Marsh and Staunton.

Some performance numbers are better than others. There are laggards – such as Austria, Italy, and Belgium – alongside the winners, like the United States, South Africa, and Australia. Japan's long-run returns are respectable despite the appalling performance following the 1980s bubble. If you invested all of your money in Austria or Italy over the long haul you would be kicking yourself. If you invested all of your money in South Africa or the United States you would be congratulating yourself. The hard part about investing is it's not easy to pick the winners or losers in advance.

Japan's stock market returns from the 1989 peak have been grim, but the rest of the global stock market didn't skip a beat. While Japan had a measly 1.4% annual return from 1990 to 2024, the MSCI All Country World Stock Market Index, which includes those terrible results from Japan, was up roughly 8% per year in that same time frame.

Yes, your performance would have been unpleasant if you had all of your money invested in Japanese equities since 1989, but if you diversified globally you would have done just fine. It's a testament to the global stock market that other countries could pick up the slack when one of the biggest stock markets in the world goes through a multi-decade run of painful underperformance.

It would also be disingenuous to assume every investor in the Japanese stock market put all of their money to work right at the peak of the bubble at the end of 1989. Even our friend Bob from earlier in the book wouldn't be that cursed.

Another way to avoid a single point of failure is by periodically investing your money into the market at different intervals, which is logically and naturally what most investors do most of the time anyway. For example, let's say you wanted to invest $100 a month into Japan's stock market over a 30-year period. You don't get to choose when you're born, so I looked at the results for the start of each 30-year period going back to 1970.

The best-case scenario would have been starting in 1970 which, of course, included the unbelievable 20-year run through 1989. You would have invested $36,000 in total, which would have turned into nearly $400,000 by 1999.* The worst-case scenario was a starting year of 1983, which led to an ending balance of $50,000. That's not a great return over three decades of investing in risk assets, which makes sense considering multiple lost decades. These are the extremes. The average results from all 30-year investing periods starting in 1970 up to 1996 was an ending balance of around $100,000. You would have done much better investing elsewhere, but the result is not the end of the world.

Unfortunately, sometimes luck – both good and bad – in your timing has a bigger say in your investment success than you realize. It almost doesn't seem fair. That's the risk of concentrating your investments in any one strategy, asset class or region of the world. The story of Japan's stock market serves as a powerful reminder that the journey of investing rarely occurs in a straight line.

Perhaps the most valuable takeaway is the importance of adaptability. Investors who stubbornly stuck to a single strategy or market paid a steep price.

You can't predict when the inevitable long downturns will occur, but you can prepare for them in advance. If mean reversion is the law of gravity in investing, then diversification is your parachute. Japan doesn't negate the power of buy-and-hold investing over the long run. Instead, it highlights the importance of diversification to capture the long-term gains of the unexpected winners.

In the next chapter, we'll take a look at what happened when the United States went through a lost decade of its own.

---

* After 20 years you would have had more than $410,000, but the market crash in the 1990s meant you went nowhere even with an additional 10 years of contributions.

17.

THE LOST DECADES

"That's what diversification is for. It's
an explicit recognition of ignorance."

—PETER BERNSTEIN

"I DON'T REALLY KNOW anything about the company."

That was Harold Davis, a doctor who purchased shares in the Netscape IPO in 1995. He flipped those shares 10 minutes later for a minor profit.

Netscape was the first internet browser to gain mass popularity in the 1990s. A few weeks before the company went public, bankers estimated the price at around $14 per share. Then demand went crazy, causing the investment bankers to raise the price to $28 on the day of the IPO. Even that wasn't high enough. The stock opened trading at over $70 per share. Investors were thirsty for internet stocks. A stockbroker at the time told *The Wall Street Journal*, "People were desperate. The calls would come in from people saying, 'I've never opened an account before, but this one I have to own. Can someone please, please, call me back?'"

By the end of the first trading day, Netscape sported a market cap of almost $3 billion. The company had yet to make a dime in profits. Kevin Kelly, a writer for *Wired* magazine at the time, explained, "Here was a company that basically had not only no profits, but it didn't even have a suggestion of how it was going to make money."

No one cared. When technological innovation ignites the animal spirits, all bets are off. Netscape was trading at more than $170 a share by the end of 1995. The dot-com boom was off and running.* That was 1995. The rest of the decade said: Hold my beer.

The bull market of the 1980s and 1990s ended with a bang as the dot-com bubble took tech stocks to the moon. In 1999, nearly 350 stocks were up 100% or more. More than 100 stocks were up 300% or better, and an astonishing 13 stocks finished the year with gains in excess of 1,000%. The biggest winner in 1999 was Qualcomm, which gained an unbelievable 2,600%.

The dot-com bubble was one of the biggest parties in stock market history. And then the bubble went *pop*. The S&P 500 was down 50% over the ensuing three years. The Nasdaq experienced a Great Depression-level crash of more than 80%.

Surely investors learned their lesson... right?

Financial historian John Kenneth Galbraith once wrote:

For practical purposes, the financial memory should be assumed to last, at a maximum, no more than 20 years. This is normally the time it takes for the recollection of one disaster to be erased and for some variant of previous dementia to come forward to capture the financial mind. It is also the time generally required for a new generation to come on the scene, impressed, as had been its predecessors, with its own innovative genius.

---

* Microsoft's Internet Explorer browser more or less made Netscape obsolete in short order, but Netscape was still bought by America Online for $4.2 billion in 1998.

The Onion once ran a headline that read:

Recession-Plagued Nation Demands New Bubble To Invest In

The Onion is a satirical publication, but as we know, many a true word is said in jest. Sure enough, it didn't take long for Americans to conjure up another bubble just a few short years after the dot-com boom and bust. And just like in Japan, this time, it was the housing market.

The housing bubble

Americans were still licking their wounds from the stock market crash in the early 2000s so they went looking elsewhere to calm their financial nerves. Much like the 1970s, the housing market was waiting with arms wide open. From 2000 to 2006, national housing prices surged by 54% after inflation. That seven-year growth exceeded the total gains of the previous five decades *combined*.

There are a number of reasons for this. Americans became addicted to borrowing money as the economy slowed. Homeowners turned their house into a piggybank by borrowing against rising home values to fund their lifestyles. Wall Street was repacking mortgage-backed securities in unhealthy ways. Banks relaxed their lending standards. It was a confluence of events that also included low interest rates, easy access to credit, exotic mortgage loans, speculative behavior, a lack of regulatory oversight and human nature. To paraphrase Gordon Gekko from Wall Street, greed was good... until it wasn't.

There is an infamous story of a strawberry picker named Alberto Ramirez who was given a $720,000 mortgage to buy a home in California despite an annual income of just $14,000.* Banks were extending loans they had no business making, but the risks were being repackaged and sold to investors who cared more about yield than

---

* Ramirez defaulted on the loan a year and a half later.

credit quality. Homebuyers were taking on mortgages that were too big for their incomes, borrowing against them to take out even more debt and financing these purchases with adjustable-rate mortgages that became punitive as interest rates rose.

The free bowls of nickels Fred Schwed described in the run-up to the Great Depression were houses in the case of this bubble.

As always, the actions taken during a boom inevitably set up the bust. It's a tale as old as markets. The dot-com bubble led to a stock market crash. The housing bubble would lead to one of the worst economic meltdowns since the Great Depression. It also gave investors one of the worst decades in U.S. stock market history.

The lost decades

The 1930s were downright ghastly. It's hard to imagine the Great Depression will ever be topped in terms of economic pain in the modern era. The 1970s were exceedingly frustrating. Investors and consumers had nowhere to hide from sky-high inflation. However, you could make the case that the first decade of the 21st century caused the most financial upheaval because American households were more heavily invested in financial assets than ever before. Everyone had more to lose.

After the dot-com bubble popped in the spring of 2000, the S&P 500 was in a bear market for the next two-and-a-half years. The stock market slowly but surely dug out of that hole after bottoming in October 2002 and finally hit new all-time highs by mid-2007. There were just nine new highs that year by the time the market peaked in October 2007 en route to the Great Financial Crisis. The financial system teetered on the edge of collapse throughout the fall of 2008 as the banking crisis went nuclear. In a White House meeting during the worst of the crisis, President George W. Bush told staffers, "If money isn't loosened up, this sucker could go down."

In September 2008, I vividly remember a hedge fund manager

telling me and my colleagues to get as much cash out of the ATM on a Friday afternoon as we could, because the banks might not open on Monday. Lehman Brothers went under. Bailouts and takeovers were happening left and right. After plummeting 50% following the bursting of the dot-com bubble, the S&P 500 crashed 57% during the Great Financial Crisis before finally bottoming in March 2009.

The new century kicked off with a lost decade of epic proportions, bookended by two gigantic stock market crashes. From the start of 2000 through the end of 2009, the S&P 500 experienced a total return of roughly -10% (including dividends), or a loss of roughly 1% per year. The Nasdaq 100 finished the first decade of the 2000s down more than 48% in total, an annualized loss of 6.4% per year. It was ugly and caused an entire generation of buy-and-hold investors to question their love of stocks.

How could this happen?

Lost decades are a painful reminder that you don't get the risk premium without the risk. They don't happen with regularity, but lost decades are part of the deal when it comes to investing in stocks.

Some unbelievable market facts

Consider the following crazy but true facts about the financial markets:

The total return from March 1997 through the bottom of the Great Financial Crisis in March 2009 was essentially 0%. The 2008 crash incinerated a dozen years' worth of gains.

The period ending in March 2020 saw long-term government bonds beat the U.S. stock market for 25 years. From the spring of 1996 through March 2020, long-term U.S. Treasury bonds returned 8.2% annually versus a return of 8.0% per year for the S&P 500. And they did so with one-third less volatility and not a single crash.*

---

* The crash in long-term government bonds came after this glorious period when they fell more than 50% in the 2020s as interest rates shot up following the inflationary spike from the pandemic spending binge.

From 1976 through the end of 2020, the U.S. bond market, as measured by the Bloomberg Aggregate Bond Index, had just three down years out of a total of 45. Those three losses were just -2.9%, -2.0% and -0.9%. In fact, there wasn't a single double-digit drawdown over any 12-month period during that time frame. Then the bond bear market of 2022 hit with reckless abandon as interest rates and inflation spiked. The U.S. bond market would fall nearly 20% as interest rates rose precipitously to fight the post-pandemic inflation.

Gold compounded at more than 35% per year from 1970 through January 1980. That's a total return of more than 1,900%, one of the greatest decade-long runs of any asset class in history. From January 1980 through the end of 2024, gold was up a total of little more than 400% or just 3.7% per year. On an inflation-adjusted basis, gold was still below the 1980 peak until 2025.

Holding cash in a savings account would have outperformed the U.S. stock market one out of every three years, on average, since the late-1920s. However, after accounting for inflation, U.S. 1-month Treasury bills once went 68 years with a negative return after inflation.

I'm having fun with numbers here but the point remains – everything underperforms eventually.

The cycle of fear and greed

It's important to understand the emotional pendulum as it swings back and forth between fear and greed because you don't want to get into the habit of buying high and selling low. Take a look at Figure 17.1, where I show the various bull and bear market cycles over the past nine-plus decades.

Figure 17.1: The cycle of fear and greed

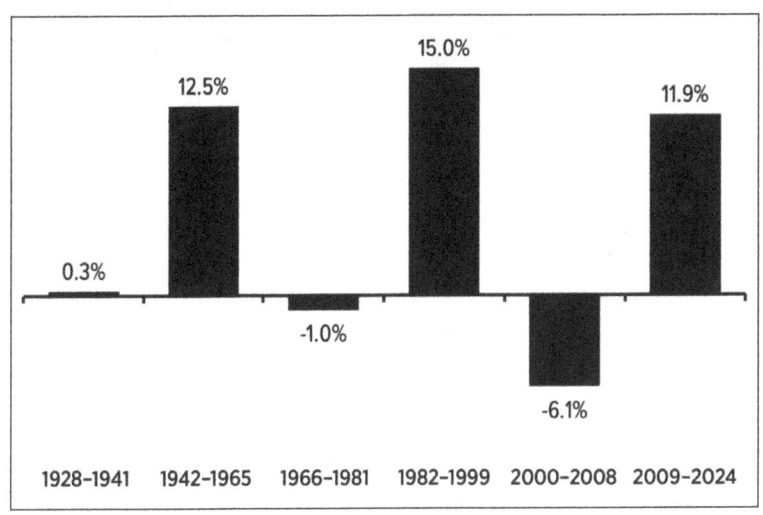

Source: Inflation-adjusted annual S&P 500 returns, NYU.

The good times and bad times can last much longer than you think, but some context is required. Sure, you can get lucky living through periods of stock market Nirvana by investing during an environment like the late 1940s through the 1950s, or the raging bull market of the 1980s and 1990s. But you don't get those rip-roaring bull markets without the prospect of stocks going nowhere or even losing money like they did from 1928 to 1941 or 1966 to 1981. Markets are always and forever cyclical.

Investing would be much easier if you could avoid the drawn-out down cycles and go all-in during the bull markets. The hard part about the timing of these cycles is that no one really knows what the difference between a cyclical (short-term) and secular (long-term) bull market is in real time.

When the 1987 Black Monday crash caused the stock market to fall more than 20% in a single day, investors thought we were going into another depression. No one could have known the bull market still had another dozen years left to run at the time. The incredible bull market that started in the 1940s kicked off during the height of the Second World War. From 1942 to 1965, there were 13 separate double-digit corrections in the U.S. stock market, including four bear markets with losses in excess of 20%. These were countercyclical drawdowns within the context of a broader bull market. Two steps forward, one step back.

The terrible times have their moments too. During the inflation of the 1970s, the S&P 500 was up more than 260% in total from 1975 to 1980. Sandwiched between the dot-com crash and the Great Financial Crisis was a respectable 80% total return – 12.7% annualized – from 2003 to 2007. The 1930s were a lost decade for investors, but the stock market was up 140% from 1933 to 1938 before taking a nosedive when the war started a year later.

The good news about lost decades is they don't happen to every asset class at the same time.

All is not lost in a lost decade

The first decade of the 21st century was downright abysmal for the S&P 500. However, large cap U.S. stocks are not the only place to invest. There are plenty of other asset classes and strategies that don't perform in line with the S&P 500 at all times. Figure 17.2 shows the total returns from 2000 to 2009 for the S&P 500 along with a handful of other asset classes and investment strategies.

Figure 17.2: Total returns from various assets/strategies (2000-2009)

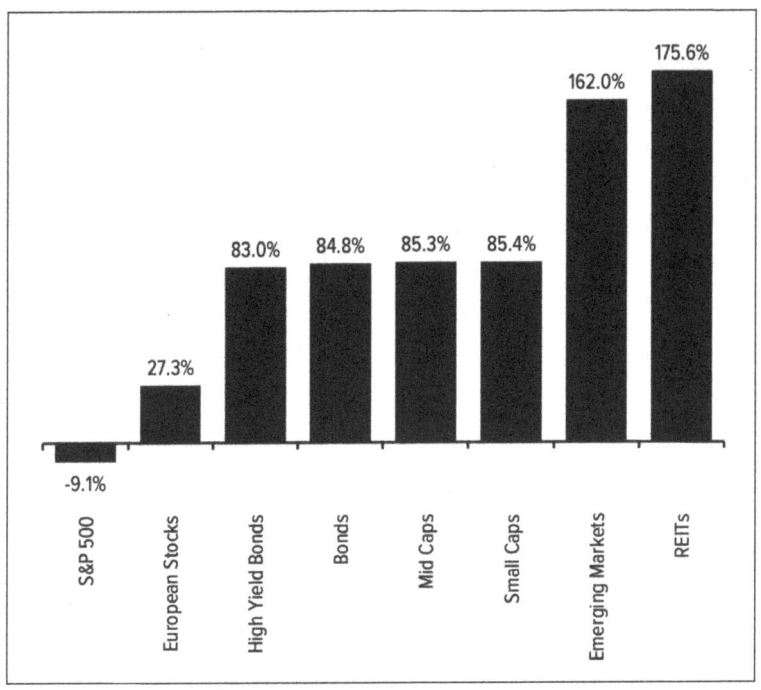

Source: Returns 2.0.

It wasn't a lost decade for bonds, small caps, mid caps, international stocks, emerging markets and real estate. Each of these asset classes performed admirably for a decade that witnessed two recessions, including one of the worst financial crises in modern times. If you had all of your eggs in the S&P 500 basket, you experienced a painful decade. You had a much smoother ride if you diversified and put those eggs in different baskets.

Howard Marks once wrote, "Here is part of the tradeoff with diversification. You must be diversified enough to survive bad times or bad luck so that skill and good process can have the chance to pay off over the long term."

Diversification is not a free lunch. But spreading your bets can help you avoid being stuck in the only strategy that experiences an extended rough patch.

In the next chapter, we'll look at some of the ways you can protect yourself from markets that go nowhere for an extended period of time.

18.

THE PERFECT PORTFOLIO

"It is better to be vaguely right
than exactly wrong."

—CARVETH READ

W HEN ORVILLE WRIGHT was in first grade, he would often
tinker with pieces of wood at his desk. His first-grade teacher
once asked what he was up to. Wright told her he was designing a
machine that he and his brother, Wilbur, would use to fly someday.
She patted him on the head and smiled politely. Little did she know.

Just five people showed up to watch the Wright brothers take their
legendary flight on December 17, 1903 in Kitty Hawk, NC. The Flyer
contained two propellers positioned between the wings. It rode on
skids that were launched on a single wooden track that acted much
like railroad tracks. The wire used to make the wings came from the
same material used to make the Brooklyn Bridge. They used some
cloth to cover the wings. There was a tiny one-gallon gas tank. Total
time in the air on the first successful attempt was estimated at just
12 seconds. On the fourth try, they made it nearly a half mile for a
one-minute flight. Their grade school dream became a reality.

Before taking that groundbreaking first flight, the Wright brothers conducted hundreds of test runs. Over four years, they faced skepticism, harsh weather, difficult conditions, injuries, remote locations, and plenty of crashes. While Wilbur and Orville had confidence in their design, they always brought reinforcements in case things didn't go as planned. They carried extra parts for their flyers – not due to a lack of faith in their piloting or building skills, but because they knew setbacks were inevitable. The spare parts served as a backup plan to ensure they could keep moving forward in the event things went wrong.

That's not to say they weren't risk-takers. Wilbur once stated, "If one were looking for perfect safety, one would do well to sit on the fence and watch the birds. But if you really wish to learn, you must mount a machine and become acquainted with its tricks by actual trial." They simply had a plan for managing the risks they were taking because they knew crashes were going to happen. Call it risk management. Call it hope for the best but plan for the worst. Call it a hedge. **The Wright Brothers were practicing diversification**. To make it to the long term (flying an airplane) they had to survive the short term (the occasional crash).

Diversification comes at a cost – there are no guarantees. You never know when it will be necessary. All those extra parts could have been a waste of time, money and valuable storage space for the Wright brothers. But they knew it was wise to avoid putting all of your planes in one basket, so to speak.

The same is true of your portfolio. Spreading your bets does not guarantee better results. In fact, it guarantees you will always have something in your portfolio that underperforms and causes consternation. In the 1970s movie *Love Story*, Ali MacGraw plays Jennifer Cavilleri, who is dying of cancer. In a classic line MacGraw tells Oliver Barrett, played by Ryan O'Neal, "Love means never having to say you're sorry." The opposite is true of diversification. Financial writer Brian Portnoy once observed, "Diversification means *always* having to say you're sorry."

If you could predict the future there would be no reason to diversify, but no one has a crystal ball that tells you what comes next in the markets. Legendary investor John Templeton once said, "The only investors who shouldn't diversify are those who are right 100% of the time." Investing involves trade-offs. Diversification is about giving up the ability to hit a home run so you don't strike out at the plate. It's about accepting good enough returns to avoid the potential for terrible returns at an inopportune time. Diversification is not undefeated, but it's never gotten blown out either.

The lost decade

Indeed, the S&P 500 went nowhere in the first decade of the 21st century. It was a terrible, horrible, no good, very bad decade. Recall from Figure 17.1 in the last chapter there were plenty of other asset classes and strategies that picked up the slack during the lost decade from 2000 to 2009. While the S&P 500 went nowhere, there were gains to be had in small caps, emerging markets, bonds, REITs, mid caps and more.

If you had all of your money in the S&P 500 it was a painful decade to say the least. If you held a diversified basket of investment strategies and asset classes, you weathered one of the worst decades in U.S. stock market history.

Now, in Figure 18.1, let's take a look at what happened in the decade *after* the lost decade for stocks.

Figure 18.1: Total returns from various assets/strategies (2010-2019)

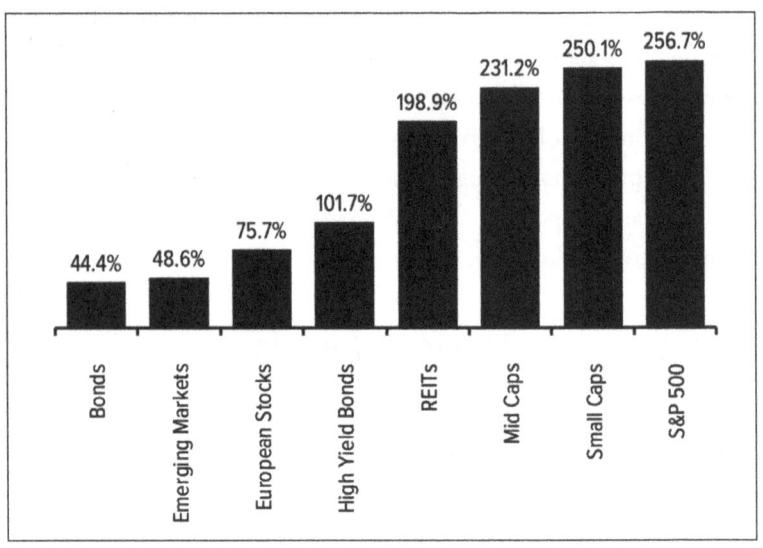

Source: Returns 2.0.

The S&P 500 went from worst to first. The cycle flipped. Many of the asset classes that outperformed in the 2000s went on to underperform in the 2010s. Some asset classes did well in both cycles. These relationships don't always work out so neatly, but the beauty of diversification is that it frees you from needing to predict the winners or losers in advance by taking the extremes off the table.

It's the decades that matter

The cycles aren't always quite as extreme as what investors experienced at the outset of the 21st century. Still, a similar dynamic exists when looking at the returns for different country stock markets around the globe – the winners and losers are constantly changing. Take a look at returns for developed country stock markets by decade going back to the 1970s, as shown in Table 18.1.

Table 18.1: Stock market total returns for developed markets by decade (1970s–2010s)

1970s		1980s		1990s	
Country	Returns	Country	Returns	Country	Returns
Japan	396.2%	Sweden	1248.4%	Sweden	464.2%
Canada	185.1%	Japan	1142.8%	USA	432.8%
France	165.6%	Italy	686.6%	UK	278.8%
Germany	164.7%	Spain	589.5%	Spain	277.5%
UK	122.4%	UK	482.2%	France	256.2%
Sweden	91.1%	France	405.3%	Germany	235.1%
USA	75.8%	USA	403.7%	Canada	155.5%
Spain	−6.2%	Germany	368.9%	Italy	123.4%
Italy	−42.7%	Canada	201.4%	Japan	−6.7%

2000s		2010s	
Country	Returns	Country	Returns
Canada	140.7%	USA	256.7%
Spain	125.3%	Sweden	112.9%
France	29.7%	Japan	92.3%
Sweden	27.0%	France	80.1%
Italy	23.2%	Germany	78.3%
Germany	20.9%	UK	64.5%
UK	14.7%	Canada	53.0%
USA	−9.1%	Italy	8.0%
Japan	−30.3%	Spain	−5.2%

Source: Returns 2.0 (MSCI Country Indexes).

Every decade, there have been big winners and big losers, with wide spreads between the winning and losing countries. The United States was near the bottom of the pack in the 1970s, 1980s and 2000s. America was one of the best-performing stock markets in the 1990s and 2010s. Pick any country on this list, and you'll find no rhyme or reason for the order in a given decade, save for the fact that no country wins or loses all the time.

Diversification is one of the best forms of risk management because it helps you avoid the extremes. Yes, that means you'll never be fully invested in the best performer, but it also means you'll never be fully exposed to the worst performer either. Diversification is a survival strategy. It might not protect you against bad years or even bad cycles. What it's meant to do is protect you against terrible decades. Every country has them.

Even the United States.

The best stocks of all time

Being diversified opens you up to surprising winners too. Peter Bernstein once observed, "I view diversification not only as a survival strategy but as an aggressive strategy, because the next windfall might come from a surprising place." This is true when it comes to owning the best stocks in the market as well. Diversification is important because the number of winning stocks over the long haul is much smaller than you think.

Hendrik Bessembinder's groundbreaking work on historical stock market returns found that just 86 companies accounted for half of all the gains in the stock market since 1926. All of the wealth created in the stock market can be attributed to around one thousand of the top-performing stocks, which is just 4% of the total. Nearly 60% of stocks failed to beat T-bill returns over their lives, while the rest barely beat a cash position.[*]

The biggest winners are all household names – Apple, Amazon, Exxon, Google, Walmart, Berkshire Hathaway, Johnson & Johnson,

---

[*] Of course, this is nearly 100 years of data. Plenty of stocks over this time had fantastic returns over shorter time frames before flaming out.

to name a few. Some people look at this data and assume it means you should just pick the best-performing stocks.

I look at this data and assume you have no chance of consistently picking those huge winners that fall into the 4% club. So you let the market pick those winners for you and own stocks via index funds to cast a wide net. This is not a sexy strategy, but it's effective.

No one knows where the big winners are going to come from. Holding concentrated positions in the stock market gives you the opportunity to outperform by a wide margin, but also increases your chances of underperforming by a wide margin. If you miss out on just a handful of the big winners you might be out of luck.

The perfect portfolio

Cartoonist Randy Glasbergen has a single-frame comic of two gentlemen sitting in a wealth management office. The client probes his advisor, "Explain to me why enjoying life when I retire is more important than enjoying life now."

This cartoon perfectly encapsulates the conflict that occupies nearly every financial decision you make in life. The essence of successful investing, retirement planning and life in general is balance. You have to plan for the future but live in the present. You have to enjoy the moment but prepare for old age. You have to invest for the long run but survive the short run. It's difficult to balance enjoying life now and ensuring you have the resources to enjoy life later.

There is no ideal balance for everyone because we all have different goals, needs, resources, expectations, and desires. The hardest part about planning for your financial future is the simple fact that you don't know what will happen. No one has it all figured out because no one knows the various curve balls life is going to throw at them. So you do the best you can. That's true when you build a portfolio too.

Vanguard founder, the late Jack Bogle, is the godfather of long-term investing. His simple yet effective investing philosophy boils down to keeping costs low and staying the course. Bogle's own portfolio was split evenly between stocks and bonds. When asked about his feelings on owning a 50/50 portfolio, Bogle admitted, "I spend about half of my time wondering why I have so much in stocks, and about half wondering why I have so little."

That's diversification for you. When creating a durable portfolio, you try to balance the following questions:

What happens if I'm right?

What happens if I'm wrong?

Harry Markowitz was the creator of Modern Portfolio Theory (MPT). Markowitz won a Nobel Prize for his work on the subject, which was the first mathematical theory used to allocate a portfolio among different asset classes based on mean-variance analysis.

That's a lot of big words and finance-speak but, essentially, the idea is to combine assets with different levels of volatility to create a portfolio that optimizes return for a given level of risk. There is a decent amount of math involved in the process, but the hope is by combining assets that act differently at different times you can create a smoother ride in your portfolio. At least that's the theory.

In plain English: diversification and asset allocation.

So did Markowitz himself go through all of the calculations in the mean-variance analysis to create the optimal portfolio on the efficient frontier with his own money? Nope. When *The Wall Street Journal's* Jason Zweig asked him how he allocated his portfolio, Markowitz admitted:

I should have computed the historical co-variances of the asset classes and drawn an efficient frontier. Instead, I visualized my grief if the stock market went way up and I wasn't in it – or if it went way down and I was completely in it. My intention was to minimize my future regret. So I split my contributions 50/50 between bonds and equities.*

Each of these titans in the finance industry could have used all sorts of fancy models to create a portfolio. Instead, they used some old-fashioned common sense and simple diversification.

I know what you're thinking.

Surely there is an optimal portfolio that will allow you to maximize your returns and minimize your risk, right? The perfect portfolio has to be out there somewhere. Someone has the ability to create a strategy that allows you to enjoy all of the upside with none of the downside, own the winners and avoid the loser and limit volatility. Where's the Holy Grail?

Alas, there is no such thing as a perfect portfolio. It only exists with the benefit of hindsight. The best you can do is find the strategy that balances the following:

- **Your risk profile**. What is your willingness, need and ability to take risk? What is your perception of risk in the markets and how does it change?
- **Your time horizon**. When are you going to spend the money? How long will your assets be invested for?
- **Your current circumstances**. Where do you stand right now in terms of your finances? How will your financial circumstances change going forward?
- **Your goals**. Where do you want to be in the future? What is the point of the money you are investing?

---

* Markowitz stated in a later interview that he had changed his tune and tried to create a more efficient, diversified portfolio. I wonder if the simple portfolio did better. I'm guessing it did.

- **Your emotional disposition**. How do you react to fear and greed? What is your relationship with emotionally charged financial decisions?

The right asset allocation – your mix of stocks, bonds, cash and other investments – is the one that offers you a high probability of achieving your goals while balancing out the potential emotional strain from gains, losses and unexpected events. Jerry Seinfeld once told Howard Stern, "Your blessing in life is when you find the torture you're comfortable with."

That's investing. It can be absolute torture at times, but there is no way around it.

George Carlin had a bit in his stand-up routine where he observed, "Have you ever noticed when you're driving that anyone who's driving slower than you is an idiot and anyone driving faster than you is a maniac?"

You have to figure out the right speed for your investments. The true perfect portfolio is the one you can stick with come hell or high water. And perfect is the enemy of good. The good strategy you can stick with is decidedly better than the perfect strategy you can't stick with.

In the Conclusion of the book, let's summarize what we've learned so far and walk through a list of ways to lose money along with my tried-and-true investment beliefs.

CONCLUSION: YOU NEED TO INVEST

"Count the perma bears on the
Forbes 400 list or the amount of
pessimists who run companies in the
Fortune 500. You will find none."

–JOSH BROWN

CANNOT IN GOOD conscience write an entire book without including at least one top 10 list.

So let's start the Conclusion with a list of 10 ways to lose money in the markets:

1. **Pretend you're smarter than the market**. Investing is easy! Outsmarting the market isn't that hard. Surely, you're more intelligent than the collective wisdom of millions of other investors, right? How hard can it really be to beat the market?
2. **Try to time the market**. Think and act in extremes. Go all in when it feels like the market is in a good place. Get out of the market when things seem dicey. Keep jumping in and out until you are poor. Anyone can do it.

3. **Chase performance**. Follow the herd. Invest with the star fund manager after the financial media falls in love with them. Follow fads. Take tips on the hottest stocks. Listen to the latest recommendation from your brother-in-law because he bought that one stock that went to the moon.

4. **Fight the last war**. Hedge the big risk that just happened. Buy the Black Swan fund after the huge crash just occurred. Invest in that inflation hedge after prices have already skyrocketed. Make the decisions you wish you would have made before you lost money. Driving in the rearview mirror feels safe so it should work just fine.

5. **Take investment advice from billionaires**. So what if billionaires have more money than you, constantly change their positioning and say stuff they don't really mean on financial television? And sure, they have no idea what your risk tolerance is and often change their minds on a dime, but they're billionaires! What's the harm in buying some puts just like George Soros or Stanley Druckenmiller?

6. **Invest only in the recent best-performing asset class**. Who cares about diversification when there is always one asset class, strategy or sector outperforming? Spend your days second-guessing why you don't have more money invested in the asset class with the best short-term performance. Take all of your money and invest it in the best performer each year. The only thing that matters is three and five-year performance numbers. If that doesn't work, buy the next one that comes along. Buy high, sell low and repeat until you're broke.

7. **Live and die by the short run**. No one has time for the long run. The sure path to riches in the markets comes from following every economic data point, earnings release, headline, financial news story and insane social media conspiracy theory you can get your hands on. You need to stay on top of this stuff so you can overreact in real-time.

8. **Sell all of your stocks in a bear market**. Bear markets are far too painful to ride out. After the market takes a nosedive, sell your

stocks and wait for the coast to clear. How hard can it be to pick bottoms? Volatility is scary. Change your portfolio constantly. Abandon your asset allocation, diversification be damned. There is no time for critical thinking. Panic first, think later.

9. **Try to get rich overnight**. Forget your goals. Delayed gratification is for losers. Take as much risk as possible to create wealth in the shortest amount of time possible. Investing is boring. Speculation is where it's at. Trade zero-day options, gamble, shoot the moon and day trade your way to riches.

10. **Don't invest in anything**. Vanguard's legendary founder Jack Bogle was once asked how investors should deal with the ever-present uncertainty involved in the world. His response was simple yet brilliant:

> Well, you can only control what you can control. I think whatever your view of the world is, you have to invest. […] The only way to guarantee you will have nothing at retirement is to invest nothing along the way. So, you have to take your chances.

Yes, risk exists in the markets. It's never going to be easy. But the alternative for stepping out into the unknown is the known of never building wealth in the first place. Don't invest. Don't save. Allow fear to control your financial decisions. Stay far away from the markets. That's a great way to ensure that your future self will be severely disappointed in you.

Even a mediocre plan is better than none.

There is a seemingly never-ending list of bad things that could happen to you as an investor. I've covered a wide range of them in this book. The true essence of investing lies in trade-offs.

When he was considering leaving a high-paying job at a hedge fund in the 1990s to start an online bookstore, Jeff Bezos used a regret minimization framework to make his decision:

> I wanted to project myself forward to age 80 and say, 'Okay, now I'm looking back on my life. I want to have minimized the number of regrets I have.' I knew that when I was 80 I was not going to regret having tried this. I was not going to regret trying to participate in this thing called the Internet that I thought was going to be a really big deal. I knew that if I failed I wouldn't regret that, but I knew the one thing I might regret is not ever having tried. I knew that that would haunt me every day, and so, when I thought about it that way it was an incredibly easy decision.

This same idea can be applied to your investing process. Some investors will regret missing out on huge gains while others will regret taking part in huge losses. Which regret will wear worse on your emotions?

How should you invest?

In every investment cycle, there comes a point where investors collectively lose their minds and insanity rules the day. During a bull market, greed is the emotional lead dog which causes investors to take far more risk than they should. During a bear market, fear takes a turn at the wheel and causes investors to panic sell.

Keeping your wits about you when others are too high or too low is not an easy task. Building a durable portfolio comes down to understanding your risk profile and time horizon, but your perception of risk constantly changes depending on the environment.

If I had to boil down investing to two simple questions, here's what I would ask:

1. When do you need the money?
2. How much can you afford to lose in the meantime, both psychologically and financially?

Every other decision stems from these two questions. The problem is that even if you can determine the answers, it's difficult to maintain the same attitude towards risk when markets and emotions are constantly changing. This is why you base your investment decisions on your goals, not the headlines.

As you benchmark your investment progress along the way there is only one question that matters:

Are you on track to reach your financial goals?

That's the biggest risk for every investor, both large and small.

What's important to recognize is that risk and reward are attached at the hip. If you cannot deal with uncertainty and volatility, you should expect to earn lower returns. If you desire higher returns, you need to become comfortable with drawdowns and unexpected events vaporizing a piece of your portfolio on occasion.

If there's one lesson this book hopes to leave you with, it's that risk cannot be avoided – it's something you have to manage, understand, and ultimately respect. The market will continue to deliver recessions, crashes, inflation, euphoria, depression and everything in between. The investors who win over time aren't the ones who predict these events – they're the ones who persist through them.

Your reward for staying the course – through the noise, the volatility, and the self-doubt – is the slow, quiet magic of compounding. Survival is the key to building wealth over the long run.

The real secret of investing, as it turns out, is no secret at all. It's the willingness to accept that pain and progress are two sides of the same coin. It's having the courage to hold when others sell, the humility to admit what you don't control and focus on what you do.

You don't need to outsmart the market. You just need to outlast it. As this book has shown time and again, the reward is worth the risk.

EPILOGUE: 20 THINGS I BELIEVE ABOUT INVESTING

To PUT A neat bow on everything you just read and be fully transparent about where I'm coming from, here are 20 things I believe about investing that can help you on your wealth-building journey.

1. **I believe simple beats complex.** The problem is that simple is much harder to implement because complex will always sound more intelligent and appealing. It's easier to be fooled by randomness with complexity. Trying harder and doing more does not guarantee better results when investing. Complexity can give you an illusion of control.

2. **I believe the timing of buy or sell decisions matters less than your holding period.** Picking tops and bottoms is for the lucky and the liars. Patiently holding onto your investments is more important for most investors than timing. Your time horizon matters more than your timing in the markets.

3. **I believe you should ignore what billionaires and legendary investors think about the markets.** These people don't share your

circumstances, time horizon or risk profile. Why should you take investing advice from them?

4. **I believe self-control can make you far more money than just about any other trait as an investor**. I know plenty of high IQ people who are terrible investors because they don't have the right temperament. Emotional intelligence and self-awareness are the attributes that separate the truly intelligent investors from those that are just well-educated.

5. **I believe every investor in risk assets should be comfortable seeing their money incinerated on occasion**. During bear markets and corrections some of your money simply vanishes. Sometimes you have to eat your losses. That's the price of admission.

6. **I believe being bullish or bearish matters less than progress towards your goals**. Your personal financial circumstances should dictate how you invest far more than what you think will happen in the markets. You don't always need to have an opinion on whether markets are going higher or lower in the short run. No one knows what will happen so you're better off preparing than predicting.

7. **I believe process is more important than outcomes, but at some point performance matters**. A successful investment process requires making good decisions over and over again. But you have to understand the difference between discipline and delusion if your process isn't working.

8. **I believe a good strategy you can stick with is vastly superior to a great one you can't stick with**. Benjamin Graham once wrote, "To achieve satisfactory investment results is easier than most people realize; to achieve superior results is harder than it looks." Perfect is the enemy of good when it comes to investment behavior.

9. **I believe it's basically impossible to forecast the economy**. Even the Fed can't figure out the path of interest rates, inflation and economic growth and it's part of their job. If we're being honest, no one truly understands how the economy works, when the next recession is coming or how long the expansions will last.

10. **I believe it's much easier to explain what just happened than predict what will happen next**. The only constants in finance are human nature and moving the goalposts when you're wrong. Pundits are very good at telling you why something unexpected was obvious in hindsight even when all of their predictions about the future have been wrong.

11. **I believe defining what you won't invest in is more important than what you will invest in.** Investors have never had it better, but the paradox of choice can be paralyzing. You can find liberation by limiting yourself to certain types of investments and ignoring everything else.

12. **I believe there are many different paths to being a successful investor, but only a handful of ways to fail**. There is no one-size-fits-all when it comes to investing the right way. But unsuccessful investors typically exhibit the same poor investment behavior – market timing, overtrading, trying to outsmart the market, being overconfident in your investment abilities, investing based on political beliefs, etc.

13. **I believe markets are right most of the time but not all the time. Markets are kind of, sort of efficient.** But just because markets can be crazy at times doesn't mean it's easy to beat them. Meir Statman once wrote, "The market might be crazy, but that doesn't make you a psychologist."

14. **I believe fighting the last war can get you into trouble**. The next risk is rarely like the last risk. I watched plenty of investors prepare for a crash for a decade following the Great Financial Crisis only to miss out on a generational bull market.

15. **I believe every investor has their own behavioral blindspots**. Knowing your lesser self is more important than worrying about what other investors are up to.

16. **I believe a long time horizon is the ultimate equalizer in the markets**. A long enough time horizon is the best hedge against most market risks.

17. **I believe doing nothing is the best investment decision most of the time**. As long as you have a plan in place, doing nothing is perfectly rational investment behavior.

18. **I believe useful investment advice is nearly impossible to accept during booms and busts**. No one wants to hear about being responsible during a rip-roaring bull market just like no one wants to hear about the virtues of buy and hold during a soul-crushing bear market.

19. **I believe most disagreements about markets come down to differences in time horizon and risk tolerance**. Markets are full of people with different goals, opinions, time horizons and appetite for risk. That's what makes a market. It's also what causes arguments and why there is always a buyer for every seller.

20. **I believe optimists are better investors than pessimists**. They say hope is not an investment strategy, but in a way, it is. If you don't think things will be better in the future than they are today, what's the point of investing in the first place?

ENDNOTES

Chapter 1

Anna Robuck, "How Shark Week hurts the very creatures it celebrates," Massive Science (July 25, 2017), www.massivesci.com.

Chapter 2

Ian Crouch, "Is Martin Short the Greatest Talk-Show Guest of All Time?" The New Yorker (March 7, 2018), www.newyorker.com.

David Marchese, "In Conversation: Martin Short," *Vulture*, www.vulture.com/2018/02/martin-short-in-conversation.html.

Jerry Seinfeld, *Is This Anything?* (Simon & Schuster, 2020).

Michael Bar-Eli, Ofer H. Azar, Ilana Ritovc, et al, "Action bias among elite soccer goalkeepers: The case of penalty kicks," *Journal of Economic Psychology* (2007), pluto.huji.ac.il/~msiritov/BarEliAzarRitovKeidarSchein.pdf.

Chapter 3

Peter Bernstein, Against the Gods: *The Remarkable Story of Risk* (Wiley 2007).

"Business Booms and Depressions since 1775," fraser.stlouisfed.org/files/docs/publications/1943chart_busibooms.pdf.

Robert J. Samuelson, *The Great Inflation and Its Aftermath: The Past and Future of American Affluence* (Random House Trade, 2010).

"When Truckers Shut Down American to Protest Oil Prices" (January 7, 2019), www.history.com/news/oil-crisis-1973-truck-strike.

"Rioting Follows Protests by Truckers in Levittown" (June 26, 1979), www.nytimes. com/1979/06/26/archives/rioting-follows-protests-by-truckers-in-levittown-pa-34-communities.html.

"Paul A. Volcker, Fed Chairman Who Wages War on Inflation is Dead at 92" (December 19, 2019), www.nytimes.com/2019/12/09/business/paul-a-volcker-dead.html.

Marty Steinberg, "Paul Volcker, the Carter-Reagan Fed chairman who beat inflation, dies at age 92" (December 9, 2019) www.cnbc.com/2019/12/09/paul-volcker-the-carter-reagan-fed-chairman-who-beat-inflation-dies-at-92.html.

Time, (December 14, 1970), content.time.com/time/magazine/0,9263,7601701 214,00.html.

www.jstor.org/stable/183891.

Chapter 4

Benjamin Roth, *The Great Depression: A Diary* (Publicaffairs, 2010).

Amy Scott, "Why do we have a 30-year mortgage, anyway?" (November 1, 2018), www.marketplace.org/2018/10/31/why-do-we-have-30-year-mortgage-anyway/.

Iqbal Khan and Robert Karofsky, "Global Wealth Report 2024," www.ubs. com/content/dam/assets/wm/global/insights/doc/global-wealth-report. pdf?campID=UC:E:601227:601243:275609551:0:1662290115:1661963018:en: 665757333.

Chapter 5

Warren E. Buffett, "Buy American. I Am," (October 16, 2008), www.nytimes. com/2008/10/17/opinion/17buffett.html.

Roger Lowenstein, *Buffett: The Making of an American Capitalist* (Random House Inc., 1995).

Joe Nocera, *A Piece of the Action: How the Middle Class Joined the Money Class* (Simon & Schuster, 2013).

Frederick Lewis Allen, *Since Yesterday: The 1930s in America, September 3, 1929– September 3, 1939* (Open Road Media, 2015).

Chapter 6

Jason Zweig, "The Psychologist Who Turned the Investing World on Its Head" (March 29, 2024), www.wsj.com/finance/investing/daniel-kahneman-behavioral-economics-270c9797.

Daniel Kahneman, "Maps of Bounded Rationality: A Perspective on Intuitive Judgment and Choice" (December 8, 2002), www.nobelprize.org/uploads/2018/06/kahnemann-lecture.pdf.

Chapter 7

Federal Reserve Bank of St. Louis, "How Bad Was the Great Depression? Gauging the Economic Impact," www.stlouisfed.org/the-great-depression/curriculum/economic-episodes-in-american-history-part-3#:~:text=The%20U.S.%20economy%20shrank%20by,%25%3B%20wholesale%20prices%20plummeted%2032%25.

Benjamin Roth, *The Great Depression: A Diary* (Publicaffairs, 2010).

Frederick Lewis Allen, *Since Yesterday: The 1930s in America, September 3, 1929–September 3, 1939* (Open Road Media, 2015).

John Kenneth Galbraith, *The Great Crash* (Penguin 2009).

John Brooks, *Once in Golconda: A True Drama of Wall Street 1920-1938* (Wiley, 1999).

Martin Fridson, *It Was a Very Good Year: Extraordinary Moments in Stock Market History* (Wiley, 2007).

Chapter 8

Robert Kurson, *Rocket Men: The Daring Odyssey of Apollo 8 and the Astronauts Who Made Man's First Journey to the Moon* (Random House Trade, 2019).

Henry S. F. Cooper Jr., *Thirteen: The Apollo Flight That Failed* (Open Road Integrated Media, Inc., 2018).

Charles Fishma, *One Giant Leap: The Untold Story of How We Flew to the Moon* (Simon & Schuster, 2020).

Charles Perrow, *Normal Accidents: Living with High Risk Technologies* (Princeton Paperbacks, 1999).

Fred Schwed, *Where Are the Customers' Yachts?* (Wiley, 2005).

Chapter 9

Benjamin Graham, *The Intelligent Investor: The Definitive Book on Value Investing* (Harper Business, 2003).

Nick Murray, *Simple Wealth, Inevitable Wealth* (1999).

William J. Bernstein, *The Four Pillars of Investing: Lessons for Building a Winning Portfolio*, (McGraw Hill, 2002).

Chapter 10

Josh Wingrove, "Forecast or US Recession Within Year Hits 100% in Blow to Biden" (October 17, 2022), www.bloomberg.com/news/articles/2022-10-17/forecast-for-us-recession-within-year-hits-100-in-blow-to-biden.

Jeff Cox, "Jeff Bezos is the latest to warn on the economy, saying it's time to 'batten down the hatches'" (October 19, 2022), www.cnbc.com/2022/10/19/amazon-founder-jeff-bezos-warns-its-time-to-batten-down-the-hatches.html.

Sam Meredith, "'This is serious': JPMorgan's Jamie Dimon warns U.S. likely to tip into recession in six to nine months" (October 10, 2022), www.cnbc.com/2022/10/10/jpmorgan-jamie-dimon-warns-us-likely-to-tip-into-recession-soon.html.

Robert Huebscher, "Gundlach: U.S. Will Face Recession by Mid-2023" (December 7, 2022), www.advisorperspectives.com/articles/2022/12/07/gundlach-u-s-will-face-recession-by-mid-2023.

Patti Domm, "Why Everyone Thinks a Recession is Coming in 2023" (December 23, 2022), www.cnbc.com/2022/12/23/why-everyone-thinks-a-recession-is-coming-in-2023.html.

"Unemployment Rate and Recessions since 1948," www.nber.org/research/business-cycle-dating.

"The Folly of Certainty" (July 17, 2024), www.oaktreecapital.com/insights/memo/the-folly-of-certainty.

Chapter 11

Gregory Suckerman, "For One GameStop Trader, the Wild Ride Was Almost as Good as the Enormous Payoff," February 3, 2021), www.wsj.com/articles/for-one-gamestop-trader-the-wild-ride-was-almost-as-good-as-the-enormous-payoff-11612348200?mod=markets_lead_pos10.

Fernando Chague, Fernando Chague, Bruno Giovannetti, "Day Trading for a Living?" (July 22, 2019), papers.ssrn.com/sol3/papers.cfm?abstract_id=3423101.

Brad M. Barber, Yi-Tsung Lee, Yu-Jane Liu, et al, "Do Day Traders Rationally Learn About Their Ability?" (October 2017), faculty.haas.berkeley.edu/odean/papers/Day%20Traders/Day%20Trading%20and%20Learning%2020110217.pdf.

"Almost 80% of Private Day Traders Lose Money" (August 17, 2016), www.curiousgnu.com/day-trading

Jason Zweig, *Your Money and Your Brain: How the New Science of Neuroeconomics Can Help Make You Rich* (Simon & Schuster, 2008).

Brian Wansink and Collin R. Payne, "Eating Behaviour and Obesity at Chinese Buffets" (September 6, 2012), onlinelibrary.wiley.com/doi/full/10.1038/oby.2008.286.

Brian Wansink, *Mindless Eating: Why We Eat More Than We Think* (Hay House UK, 2001).

"The real winners and losers in America's lottery obsession" (January 4, 2023), https://www.nprillinois.org/2023-01-04/the-real-winners-and-losers-in-americas-lottery-obsession.

Chapter 12

"2024 Commencement Address by Roger Federer" (June 9, 2024), home.dartmouth.edu/news/2024/06/2024-commencement-address-roger-federer.

Chapter 13

Brad Stone, *The Everything Store: Jeff Bezos and the Age of Amazon* (Corgi, 2014).

Frederick Lewis Allen, *Since Yesterday: The 1930s in America, September 3, 1929–September 3, 1939* (Open Road Media, 2015).

Joe Nocera, *A Piece of the Action: How the Middle Class Joined the Money Class* (Simon & Schuster, 2013).

Investment Company Institute and the Securities Industry Association, "Equity Ownership in America" (Fall, 1999), www.ici.org/system/files/attachments/rpt_equity_owners.pdf.

Chapter 15

Ruth Youngblood, "A deluge of fraudulent loans has jolted Japan's banking…" (September 1, 1991, www.upi.com/Archives/1991/09/01/A-deluge-of-fraudulent-loans-has-jolted-Japans-banking/5143683697600/.

Alexandra Bregman, "Forgotten boom: the legacy of Japan's 1980s art buying spree" October 16, 2020), asia.nikkei.com/Life-Arts/Arts/Forgotten-boom-the-legacy-of-Japan-s-1980s-art-buying-spree2.

Ben Carlson, "The Biggest Asset Bubble in History" (May 11, 2023), awealthofcommonsense.com/2023/05/the-biggest-asset-bubble-in-history/.

"Court sentences Onoue to 12 years for fraud" (March 2, 1998), www.japantimes.co.jp/news/1998/03/02/national/court-sentences-onoue-to-12-years-for-fraud/.

Leslie Helm, "Ex-Hostess in Japan's Bank Scandal Is Shadowy Figure" (September 16, 1991), www.latimes.com/archives/la-xpm-1991-09-16-fi-1678-story.html.

Christopher Wood, *The Bubble Economy: Japan's Extraordinary Speculative Boom of the '80s and the Dramatic Bust of the '90s* (Equinox Publishing, 2005).

Charles Kindleberger, *Manias, Panics and Crashes by Charles Kindleberger* (Palgrave Macmillan, 2023).

"This Japanese Shop is 1020 Years Old" (January 7, 2021), www.nytimes.com/2020/12/02/business/japan-old-companies.html.

Chapter 16

Henry K. Beeche, "The Powerful Placebo" (December 24, 1955), www.dcscience.net/beecher-placebo-1955.pdf.

"Is the Placebo Powerless? – An Analysis of Clinical Trials Comparing Placebo with No Treatment" (May 24, 2001), www.nejm.org/doi/full/10.1056/NEJM200105243442106.

Daniel Kahneman, *Thinking, Fast and Slow* (Penguin, 2012).

"UBS Global Real Estate Bubble Index 2025," www.credit-suisse.com/about-us-news/en/articles/news-and-expertise/global-investment-returns-yearbook-2023-202302.html.

Chapter 17

Molly Baker "Technology Investors Fall Head Over Heels for Their New Love" (August 10, 1995), www.wsj.com/articles/SB108203965398683708.

Adam Lashinsky, "Netscape IPO 20-year anniversary: Read Fortune's 2005 oral history of the birth of the web" (August 9, 2015), fortune.com/2015/08/09/remembering-netscape/.

Eric Niiler, "Netscape's IPO Anniversary and the Internet Boom" (August 9, 2005), www.npr.org/2005/08/09/4792365/netscapes-ipo-anniversary-and-the-internet-boom.

John Kenneth Galbraith, *A Short History of Financial Euphoria* (Penguin Business, 1994).

Anthony Ha, "Minorities Hit Hard by Foreclosure Crunch" (May 3, 2007), sanbenito.com/minorities-hit-hard-by-foreclosure-crunch/.

Chapter 18

David McCullough, *The Wright Brothers* (Simon & Schuster, 2015).

"Do stocks outperform Treasury bills?" wpcarey.asu.edu/department-finance/faculty-research/do-stocks-outperform-treasury-bills.

Jason Zweig, "Jack Bogle's Bogleheads Keep Investing Simple. You Should Too" (October 5, 2018), www.wsj.com/articles/jack-bogles-bogleheads-keep-investing-simple-you-should-too-1538754027.

Jason Zweig, "What Harry Markowitz Meant" (November 7, 2025), jasonzweig.com/what-harry-markowitz-meant.

ABOUT THE AUTHOR

Ben Carlson, CFA is the Director of Institutional Asset Management at Ritholtz Wealth Management and advocates long-term investment strategies. He is the author of four previous books including *Everything You Need To Know About Saving For Retirement.* He is also the creator of the blog *A Wealth of Common Sense* which breaks down wealth management and financial markets. Ben is also the co-host of the popular *Animal Spirits* podcast which has previously been named in *Fortune*'s Best Business Podcasts.